Elements in Christian Doctrine
edited by
Rachel Muers
University of Edinburgh
Ashley Cocksworth
University of Roehampton
Simeon Zahl
University of Cambridge

A THEOLOGY OF HOME IN A TIME OF HOMELESSNESS

Siobhán Garrigan
Trinity College Dublin

Shaftesbury Road, Cambridge CB2 8EA, United Kingdom

One Liberty Plaza, 20th Floor, New York, NY 10006, USA

477 Williamstown Road, Port Melbourne, VIC 3207, Australia

314–321, 3rd Floor, Plot 3, Splendor Forum, Jasola District Centre, New Delhi – 110025, India

103 Penang Road, #05–06/07, Visioncrest Commercial, Singapore 238467

Cambridge University Press is part of Cambridge University Press & Assessment, a department of the University of Cambridge.

We share the University's mission to contribute to society through the pursuit of education, learning and research at the highest international levels of excellence.

www.cambridge.org
Information on this title: www.cambridge.org/9781009566292

DOI: 10.1017/9781009566339

© Siobhán Garrigan 2025

This publication is in copyright. Subject to statutory exception and to the provisions of relevant collective licensing agreements, with the exception of the Creative Commons version the link for which is provided below,no reproduction of any part may take place without the written permission of Cambridge University Press & Assessment.

An online version of this work is published at doi.org/10.1017/9781009566339 under a Creative Commons Open Access license CC-BY-NC 4.0 which permits re-use, distribution and reproduction in any medium for non-commercial purposes providing appropriate credit to the original work is given and any changes made are indicated. To view a copy of this license visit https://creativecommons.org/licenses/by-nc/4.0

When citing this work, please include a reference to the DOI 10.1017/9781009566339

First published 2025

A catalogue record for this publication is available from the British Library

ISBN 978-1-009-56629-2 Hardback
ISBN 978-1-009-56628-5 Paperback
ISSN 2977-0211 (online)
ISSN 2977-0203 (print)

Cambridge University Press & Assessment has no responsibility for the persistence or accuracy of URLs for external or third-party internet websites referred to in this publication and does not guarantee that any content on such websites is, or will remain, accurate or appropriate.

For EU product safety concerns, contact us at Calle de José Abascal, 56, 1°, 28003 Madrid, Spain, or email eugpsr@cambridge.org

A Theology of Home in a Time of Homelessness

Elements in Christian Doctrine

DOI: 10.1017/9781009566339
First published online: April 2025

Siobhán Garrigan
Trinity College Dublin
Author for correspondence: Siobhán Garrigan, garrigs@tcd.ie

Abstract: Homelessness abounds today in various forms of displacement and as a pervasive condition of unbelonging. It ruins health, lives, communities, habitats, creativity, and hope. This Element argues that for theology to play its part in ending homelessness, it must better understand its own concept of 'home'. The Element proposes a vision of home capable of resisting the tacit, mistaken theology of home that undergirds the various iterations of modern homelessness. Weaving biblical and ritual sources, the argument constructs theological responses to the twin forces of capitalism and nationalism which, alloyed with sexism and racism, constitute the time of homelessness in which we live. It asks the reader to imagine home as 'participating instead of possessing' in every sphere of life, in pursuit of a theology of home aimed at preventing homelessness and not merely ministering to people experiencing it. This title is also available as Open Access on Cambridge Core.

Keywords: homelessness, participation, theology, sacramentality, nationalism

© Siobhán Garrigan 2025

ISBNs: 9781009566292 (HB), 9781009566285 (PB), 9781009566339 (OC)
ISSNs: 2977-0211 (online), 2977-0203 (print)

Contents

	Introduction	1
1	Home as Participation in the Life of God	8
2	Discipleship	23
3	Companionship	33
4	Sacramentality	44
	Conclusion	53
	References	60

Introduction

Homelessness is not new. In mid twentieth-century England, both my parents experienced homelessness as children and my great-uncle, who died in Northampton in 1990 had, like many Irish people living in England, experienced long periods of homelessness. In all the hostels and other projects for people experiencing homelessness in which I worked from 1987 to 1997 in the UK, the United States, and Ireland, there were always more people seeking access than could be accommodated. And of course, long before the twentieth century, the world's poorer people were always vulnerable to homelessness, just as were those displaced by war, famine, climate change, and other disasters. Why then is the current era, the early twenty-first century, said to be one of homelessness?

The prevalence of homelessness today is often expressed in terms of numbers. In 2024, refugees number 43.4 m globally and 63.3 m more people are internally displaced, with a further 12.7 m seeking asylum or international protection (UNHCR, 2024). These numbers, though high, are in fact comparable to Europe after World War II, where over 40 m people were refugees, a further 13 m ethnic Germans were expelled from the Soviet Union and in Eastern Europe, one million residents of the Soviet states fled the nascent totalitarianism. In addition, a further 11.3 m displaced foreigners were found inside Germany and millions of Germans had fled the advancing Soviet army (UNHCR, 2000). However, the difference for the twenty-first century is that, unlike the post-war scenario, these figures are expected to go up not down, and massively so, due to wars and the climate crisis. Indeed, it is estimated that between 2025 and 2050, climate change alone will drive up to 1.2 billion people from their homes (UNHCR, 2024).

In the cities of Ireland, the UK and the United States, the number of people experiencing homelessness has also been rising significantly, with little evidence of reductions on the horizon. In Ireland, the number of people experiencing homelessness has increased up to threefold in the past decade alone (Focus Ireland, 2024), and in the UK, street-sleeping is up 120 per cent over the past fifteen years (Crisis, 2024). Street-sleeping in cities may colloquially be equated with 'the homeless', but the majority of people experiencing homelessness are in emergency or temporary accommodation, where numbers are rising steadily – including in the United States, where the 40 per cent increase in the past decade has disproportionately affected African Americans and seniors (Ludden, 2023). At the same time, the number of people experiencing 'hidden' homelessness has also greatly increased and looks set to continue to do so, especially in rural communities. Hidden homelessness takes forms that particularly affect women and children: sofa-surfing, car-dwelling, continuous-visiting, squatting (Cloke, 2002; Simon, 2022). Although all the aforementioned phenomena are termed 'temporary displacement', and most people's experiences of homelessness are relatively short (O'Sullivan, 2020), even a brief period of homelessness can have devastating effects (Parekh, 2016).

Numbers alone can distract from the human dimensions of this devastation. Humans need housing and the consequences of lacking it are well documented (Lee, 2021). Homelessness produces acute anxiety, isolation, pain, diminished health, reduced life expectancy, interrupted/suspended education, lack of opportunity for productive work, depression, and increased vulnerability to discrimination and attack. Moreover, the longer homelessness lasts, the more consequential are its effects.

Homelessness can also be said to characterise today's world because so many people's lives are blighted by stress induced by the *threat* of it. This happens, for example, when a tenancy is ending and tenants cannot find or afford a new rental, when pensions do not keep pace with inflation and older tenants face eviction because they cannot pay rising rents, when people live in poverty because their income is consumed by housing costs, or when people must live with their parents until their late forties or fifties (because both renting and house-purchasing are unaffordable). As well as stress, the latter situation carries serious implications for personal development, relationships, and parenting choices.

Homelessness also weakens democratic processes, because it has negative effects on politics as well as individual well-being. For instance in Ireland, the past decade's 'housing crisis' (caused by the privatisation of the housing market, profiteering development policies, and rents rising faster than wages) has negatively affected large numbers of Irish residents who do not have the housing they need, but it has also fuelled the growing popularity of far-right political groups who deploy the argument that there is no available housing as a rationale for anti-immigration politics. Ireland shares this and other political consequences of homelessness with the UK and many other industrialised countries, even as the driving causative factors of homelessness vary with context. Reacting to the growth in homelessness and its consequences for both individuals and politics across the European Union, the Member States in 2021 agreed to the Lisbon Declaration on Combating Homelessness. Its goal is that by 2030

> no one sleeps rough for lack of accessible, safe and appropriate emergency accommodation; no one lives in emergency or transitional accommodation longer than is required for successful move-on to a permanent housing solution; no one is discharged from any institution (e.g. prison, hospital, care facility) without an offer of appropriate housing; evictions should be

prevented whenever possible and no one is evicted without assistance for an appropriate housing solution, when needed; and no one is discriminated against due to their being homeless. (European Commission, 2021)

Ireland, at least, will struggle to realise this goal because it does not have the one thing that research repeatedly has shown is needed to accomplish it: 'a sufficient level of affordable and secure housing' (O'Sullivan, 2022: 4). Why do we not have this? Partly because of the lack of political will to create it: successive neoliberal governments have sold off the social housing stock, favoured the private sector (through development privileges, tax breaks, and tourism – AirBnB having removed rental stock), and been slow to adopt a 'housing first' approach to combating homelessness (Adams, 2022). Another factor is what Kevin Hargaden identifies as the normalisation of greed, and the absence of voices willing to name it as such (Hargaden, 2021). But the lack is also due to a commonly held perception of the sorts of activities demanded in the Lisbon Declaration as the preserve of 'charity' rather than the state, predicated on a normative perception of the homeless person as other – lesser, a failure of sorts.

At the root of all three factors (housing stock, private profit, and 'charitable' attitudes) are a number of conceptual problems. How people think about housing and homelessness is not a given; it is a construct, a set of ideas. Of course, homelessness is experienced and threatened differently according to culture and region; sleeping on friends' sofas for a year 'means' homelessness in one context but not in others. Homelessness is also far from a singular experience, taking multiple forms within and across different regions and cultures – inevitably, given that the drivers of homelessness are historical, political, cultural and fundamentally spatial, as well as uniquely personal (Cloke, 2010). But at the root of these various forms of homelessness are ideas about what constitutes a home. This Element challenges the dominant idea of home in the West today, because the measures that need to be taken to accomplish the goal of ending homelessness will depend on altered ideas about home. It does so by appeal to theology because, it contends, the operational idea of home in the West was formed by Christian ideas.

Turn on the television any night of the week, and there is a plethora of programmes about the Western idea of home, from buying or building one, through decorating or renovating one, to selling or demolishing one: Great British Home Restoration, Owning Manhattan, Incredible Homes, Room to Improve, Escape to the Country, Grand Designs, and many more. Corresponding advertisements bombard viewers with data on how to find, finance, and fill their home, all while housing insecurity imposes devastating financial, physical, and emotional tolls on many people. I suspect the question posed by the television, 'What ought a home to look like, feel like, consist of?' is so appealing because it contains within it the trace of a deeper one: 'How can I *be at home* in this precarious world?' Such a question bespeaks the existential alongside the pragmatic dimensions of this time of homelessness.

It is existential homelessness alongside material homelessness that affords the current age its title in this Element. Describing homelessness as the very condition of modernity, Peter Berger identified a psychological wound in the West inflicted by modernity's relentless stripping people of ties that had, for millennia, forged their sense of belonging. So extensive was the spatial and spiritual rootlessness thus caused that Berger said it constituted a 'metaphysical loss of "home"' (1974: 82). Similarly, homelessness has been said to characterise our age because of the 'liquidity' of late modernity; the ways, as Zygmunt Bauman described them, once 'solid' social foundations (such as religion, marriage, employment) became optional, malleable, or unreliable, rendering humans 'tourists' where once they were 'pilgrims' through their own lives (2000). More recently, however, various studies have argued that to remark homelessness as merely one of modernity's effects does not go far enough. Achille Mbembe's identification of 'surplus populations' reveals people displaced by political oppression and climate change, and whole species denied their habitats, as the essential conduits of today's 'necropolitics' rather than their collateral damage (2019). Homelessness is thus increasingly seen as a key *technique* of twenty-first-century global, neoliberal politics because it is essential to the nexus of capitalism, corporate extractivism, racism, and sexism on which it relies.

By contrast, nihilism suggests homelessness is not a product of a peculiarly contemporary geo-politics but, rather, characteristic of human nature. Humans are restless, the argument goes, because they are born to roam, and those who feel 'at home' in a particular place are in what Martin Heidegger called a 'non-authentic' state (Colonello, 1999: 41). Accordingly, the question posed by nightly television might be portrayed as a perennial one. However, there is a lot of evidence to the contrary. Research has identified a direct link between a lack of a sense of belonging and depression, and an indirect link to suicide (e.g., Fisher et al., 2015). Moreover in Ireland, for millennia and until very recently, people, dialects, accents, and tunes were generally understood as properly belonging somewhere specific, originating from that place and serving as an expression of it. This was the product of a worldview wherein, as Patrick Kavanagh wrote, 'To know fully even one field or land is a lifetime's experience.' He added, 'In the world of poetic experience it is depth that counts, not width. A gap in a hedge, a smooth rock surfacing a narrow lane, a view of a woody meadow, the stream at the junction of four small fields – these are as much as a man [sic] can fully experience' (Kavanagh, 2003: 217 [1967]). Hundreds of thousands of accounts in the forms of letters, songs, literature, court records, and newspaper articles remain from Irish people who – like my parents' families – had to emigrate. They bear witness to the acute pain people felt at separation from their home-place; a pain one would not expect to find had they been born to roam.

It must be noted that many of these migrants found 'home' oppressive – female and queer people perhaps especially – and for them, leaving represented a certain emancipation even as it also involved pain. Furthermore, as will become apparent, I am not in favour of the idea of home as a singular entity on the earth, nor as a pure origin. The tendency to romanticise the idea of home or insist it is singular – whether imaged as a family, house, field, region, or country – is a strategy for overlooking and denying the ways that power is operational in the home and the ways that any one home is connected to other homes. Moreover, some homes are nurturing and safe while others shelter abuse and neglect. Nevertheless, the importance of a specific home-place to a sense of belonging outweighs the evidence for allegedly natural mobility, in Ireland at least, and internationally, there is also scepticism that the nihilistic view feeds into the positive touting of cosmopolitanism as one of globalisation's goods. Therefore, alongside a collective of feminist postcolonial scholars, I 'question the presumptions that rootless mobility is the defining feature of contemporary experience and that it stands against any form of "rooted belonging"' (Ahmed et al., 2003: 2).

What has created the possibility of humans being theorised as normatively rootless are the ways modernity interrupted the relationship of people with place via colonisation and industrialisation. Willie James Jennings's *The Christian Imagination* articulates the extent of what went wrong – theologically and in terms of theological anthropology – when human connection to place was severed by colonisation; he also articulates the mechanisms by which it happened. Focusing on the relationship between humans and place/land, he exposes the deep and complex ways that place/land constituted human life before colonial modernity re-imagined it as something to be possessed and managed for producing commodities, leaving humans to be imagined as mobile and rationally constituted. He suggests that the driving force of colonisation, whiteness, from the late mediaeval period until today, substitutes race for place and place-centred identity. Indeed, 'When you disrupt and destroy the delicate and contingent connection of peoples' identities bound to specific lands you leave no alternative but racial agency' (2010: 58). And he concludes that not only does sequestering land and reordering its peoples in a top-down way render the world according to racial hierarchies, but also, by severing human relationship to place, it ensures that the very mechanisms of relating are forgotten. Human-animal-plant-land relationships were symbiotic; separated and racialised, human techniques for living interrelatedly were lost.

No wonder today's world is characterised by homelessness, when modernity so thoroughly severed the fabric of human belonging – to terroir, one another, and across species. Whiteness – the process of claiming privilege as entitlement – did so specifically through segregation, reordering the built environment and land itself to keep one sort of person from another; poor from rich, Black from white, Jew from Christian, Catholic from Protestant (Garrigan, 2014). And it ensured that the lower place in the racialised hierarchy was reflected in precarious, or absent, provision for the 'lesser' peoples' needs, paramount among which, as for any people, are homes. As Jennings remarks, 'Segregation is to homelessness what waterways are to fish' (2023). Homelessness is segregation's inevitable effect. It is also a largely invisible effect, having come to seem 'natural', the way of the world, because of the ways segregation replicates itself in human self-understanding and treatment of the earth. The homelessness that characterises our era consequently also seems somehow inevitable, natural, rather than the ecological, spiritual, and humanitarian scandal it is.

Such a neutral mythology has wound its way into the very concept of 'home', such that it can be presented as a televised commodity, when in fact, as Rosemary Marangoly George remarks, thanks to colonial modernity, 'Imagining a home is as political an act as imagining a nation. Establishing either is a display of hegemonic power' (1999: 6). Segregation thus does not merely create homelessness; it embeds othering into the heart of the idea of home through its hierarchical ordering of power, top-down. Consequently, 'the basic organising principle around which the notion of "home" is built is a pattern of select inclusions and exclusions' (George, 1999: 2), meaning that homelessness is, in the current system, inevitable: for some to be at home is for others not to be so.

Homelessness has become a major area of scholarship over the past twenty years in Geography, Social Policy, Architecture, and Environmental Studies, as well as in interdisciplinary studies of migration, gender, ecology, and decolonisation. Theology has, however, given it relatively little attention. Apart from Jennings, when theology does tackle homelessness it is usually via four approaches. The first exhorts social change, using religious values to criticise prevailing social and economic policy, on the basis that systemic inequalities produce exclusion that is impossible to tackle at local level alone (e.g., Mulligan, 2023). The second nurtures ministry among those experiencing homelessness by reference to biblical and other religious sources, mining what they say about homelessness (e.g., Bouma-Prediger and Walsh, 2008).

A Theology of Home in a Time of Homelessness   7

The third listens to people experiencing homelessness and presents as primary data the information, wisdom, and theologies heard within (e.g., Nixon, 2013). Like the first approach, this third one is sometimes framed as 'liberation theology' (e.g., Costoya, 2021). And the fourth approach studies how religious communities respond to homeless people and their needs, from soup kitchens through shelters to social housing projects (e.g., Keenan and McGreevy, 2019). Approaches can be combined, as when Suzanne Mulligan outlines how Catholic Social Teaching offers potential challenges to economic policy (first) but also how 'we must learn from those who are unhoused ... through encounter and accompaniment' (third) (2023: 446). Or as when Laura Stivers, combining all four types, advocates 'prophetic disruption' to counter habitual Christian responses to homelessness which she criticises for reinforcing the dominant ideologies that cause it (Stivers, 2011).

This Element, rather than studying homelessness as a social phenomenon, approaches it by asking: what is the idea of home in Christian theology? It does so because while the homelessness that characterises our times is a social phenomenon, a material reality for people without the housing they need, it is also, as outlined earlier, existential: many albeit housed people do not feel an adequate sense of belonging to enable them to flourish. The approach taken by this Element is predicated on an understanding that material and existential homelessness are intrinsically linked, and so it asks: What is the operational idea of home such that both iterations of homelessness can be so prevalent? And how might the idea of home be re-thought so that homelessness, and its damage, can be prevented?

Where does one turn to for a theology not of homelessness but of home? At first glance, the Bible presents confusing or even contradictory views. On the one hand, there is the idea that our only home is with God in heaven. From there we came and to there we will return after death. Until then, foxes have holes, birds have nests, but the Son of Man has no place to lay down, and we are called to follow him. On the other hand, we read that having a home in this world matters: God made God's own home here, as the Creator in Creation, but also in the tabernacles in the Hebrew Bible and in the Incarnation. Moreover, the Gospels portray Jesus as far from anti-home – he uses certain homes as the base for his ministry (like Peter's Mother-in-law's or Martha and Mary's) and he sent his mother from the foot of the cross to make her home with his beloved friend.

Numerous studies have taught us how different a concept was 'household' in the biblical context of the Ancient Near East to the Anglophone 'home' that now usually translates it, and this goes some way to help understand these apparent contradictions. However, strong ideas of home are presented in the Bible, just not usually through the word 'home'. One of these, which forms the heart of this Element, is the idea of home as participation in the life of God. The following section therefore begins by conceptualising home via biblical and early church references to 'participation in the life of God'. Quite quickly it becomes apparent that how later Christianity often imagined home – as something from which earthly creatures are exiled and for which they long – separated Christians from the deep belonging promised by biblical intimations of participation in the life of God. This first section thus identifies a mistake in colloquial Christian discourse which, recognising humanity's home in God only before birth and after death, neglected its participation in God during earthly life. It proceeds to trace how this 'gap of the now' resulted in a profound human longing for 'home' and this longing in turn led people to adopt both nationalism and capitalism, to fill the gap.

If theology played a part in creating this distorted idea of home, it might yet, by reconceptualising its idea of home, play a part in dismantling it. To understand how participation in the life of God *as home* might close the gap of the now, the following three sections identify and examine three strands as constitutive of participation in divine life: discipleship (following Jesus), companionship (loving the stranger), and sacramentality (sensing God's presence). A concluding section will then draw these strands together by imagining home as a verb – participating, not possessing – to resist the time of homelessness in which we live by means of an alternative vision of home.

1 Home as Participation in the Life of God

What if home were imagined not as something one possessed, or even occupied, but as something in which one participated? This section proposes that cultivating an idea of home as participation, and particularly as participation in the life of God, has the potential to tend the wounds caused by colonial modernity's endemic reproduction of homelessness and, over time, to construct an alternative to it.

To participate is to join without owning, to improvise without controlling, to compromise while remaining true to oneself; it is to listen, to express, to create, to breathe, and to belong – contingently. To live contingently is to affirm interrelationality with the earth, across species, and between humans. It requires imagination as well as tenacity to guarantee the safety and flourishing of all participants equally, while also eschewing the temptation to perceive the static as representing security. It is to be guided by and rely upon the Spirit in all things.

This section begins by excavating the theological meaning of human participation in the life of God. It identifies a significant mistake in how participation has been interpreted within the Christian tradition, whereby earthly human life came to be understood as separated from God. It argues that this theological mistake made Christians and other inheritors of the Christian tradition particularly susceptible to nationalism and capitalism, and the section proceeds to expose how these forces have come to substitute for 'home' in today's world. It then charts a path for reclaiming – from biblical, doctrinal, and liturgical sources – the deep sense of belonging that remains available for understanding participation in the life of God *as* home.

1.1 Participation

Participation as a theological theme has waxed and waned in popularity over the centuries. In recent decades, this theme experienced something of a revival in Protestant circles due to so-called Protestant Thomism, Pauline biblical theology, and Millbankian Radical Orthodoxy. It was also central to Vatican II's reforms of Roman Catholicism, which asserted that for 'all the faithful', participation is 'their right and duty by reason of their baptism' and 'the primary and indispensable source from which [they] are to derive the true Christian spirit' (*Sacrosanctum concilium*, 14). Accordingly, Vatican II mandated the use of vernacular languages in worship, architectural alterations to bring clergy and congregation closer together, and instructions that worship leadership should enable the 'full, active, and conscious participation' of the laity.

By engendering participation as a means to more faithful relationship with God, Vatican II had much in common with the Lutheran Reformation 450 years previously, particularly its insistence on direct access to the Bible for lay people. Like that earlier movement, Vatican II's demands for aesthetic changes were not mere modernisations but corrections to profound theological missteps. Pragmatic worldly participation was directly correlated with human participation in divine life. In both reform mandates, the demand for actual, sensory, and intellectual participation was a corrective to a church that had forgotten what Augustine taught: that human destiny is actually participation in divinity and that the means by which this is accomplished is learning, forming ideas through ever-deeper encounter with and orientation to God (and not by outsourcing this relationship to clerical authorities).

Understanding human destiny *as* participation in divinity, 'deification', is a very early Christian doctrine, first formulated by Ireneaus (*Adversus haereses* 5, preface) and pithily attributed to Athanasius as: 'God became human so that humans might become God' (*De incarnatione* 54, 3). For early Church writers, the vocabulary for humans becoming God, *theopoiethomen*, carried the sense of 'participating in' rather than ontologically changing from one type of 'stuff' to another. This participatory meaning was most clearly developed by Augustine who recognised that it has a profound effect on how people experience their lives if they understand that human destiny in God, even as it has an eternal telos, very much begins on earth (Marrocco, 2000). There followed a long and ecumenical tradition of teaching that humans are meant to participate in God through their earthly experiences. However, it was not without its difficulties, and later Western thinkers let the doctrine fade from view because of the part it played in the problem, as they saw it, of the Eastern churches collapsing the Creator-creation distinction. As almost all the recent Anglophone revivals of the term admit, it is still difficult in English to say 'participating in God' without running this same risk. To try to avoid too great an ontological claim, I amend the phrase to 'participating in the life of God'.

Amending this phrase does not fully overcome the risk of Creator-creation collapse, but it is helpful for recognising both that and *how* God is active in the world, now (and always). To add 'the life of' God is to remark the ongoing vitality of God's work in the world, as well as the accessibility of that divine life to creatures, instead of having to imagine God existing 'elsewhere' in order to feel access to God. This little phrase, *the life of* God, brings attention to the here-and-now, to support the suggestion that participation in the here-and-now constitutes home for humans. The phrase does not limit divine life to creation, but it does pull a focus onto the aspect of divine life that is an immanent creation-involving life-force. As such, this Element differs considerably from the Protestant participation projects mentioned at the start of this section, whose treatments of deification aim to reinforce a metaphysical distance to God's transcendence, often in support of authoritarian theologies (Dominiak, 2020). For me, participation in 'the life of' God is an idea intended to reassure creatures in 'the life of' creatureliness, because creaturely life is that part of the life of God to which God has given humans access. This creaturely life itself is where we are part of the life of God and, thus, can be at home.

1.2 Participation in the Life of God as Creatures

Participation in the life of God can *only* happen for humans via participation in the world of which they are a part, as creatures in creation. Stories matter, and they concurrently shape individuals and communities; but they are constructs, the arts and not the authors of the biotic context that is fundamental to human life. Christian tradition, like the Jewish one in which it is based, conceives the author of this biotic context as God, and because God's creating work is understood to be *ongoing*, and not merely a heavy week's work at the start of earth-time, humans can be conceived as participants in the life of God. Indeed, it is by inhabiting this participation that they can feel at home in the world. And yet, as will be discussed, too often humans have not encountered their biotic context as participation in the life of God; the one has been separated from the other, with catastrophic consequences for creation and creatures alike – the roots of homelessness.

When talking about the divine author of creation, Christian theology has two dominant naming traditions. One is that of the Logos/Word, the sacred animating principle that derives from ancient Greek cosmologies and poetically ascribes creative agency to various forms of divine speech. The other names God 'Creator': 'the creator of heaven and earth' as the Apostles' Creed states it. 'Let all things their creator bless', exhorts the nineteenth-century hymn 'All Creatures of our God and King', echoing the Canticle of St. Francis 800 years earlier. And 'Creator God' is the term of address with which many of today's prayers begin, particularly during the recently demarcated ecumenical 'Season of Creation'. Both traditions hold as pivotal the creation narratives of the Hebrew Bible (Genesis 1), which conceive creation 'out of nothing' (and, unlike their antecedents, do not ascribe an origin story to God), while the Logos tradition, due to Paul's letters and John's Gospel, also explicitly demarcates God's creating work in Christ. Significantly, the Nicene Creed specifies God as 'Maker', enabling its distinction that Christ was 'begotten, not made', All other humans are 'made' and called to participation in the divine life; Christ is already divine.

While I argue that participation in the life of God is 'home' to humans, it is vital to note that the life of God exceeds creation and its creatures. Creation is made; God is not. And precisely because the nature and scope of God's life is greater than its presence in creation, participation can put humans in touch with a sense of something transcendent. This is not the sort of transcendence imagined by ontotheology, whereby instrumentalist measures (prayer, penance, praise) permit momentary access for an individual to divinity; it is transcendence as *intersubjectivity*, which is the condition of human participation in both creation and God.

Intersubjectivity is the claim that subjectivity is contingent on a vast complex of prior and current interrelationships. It maintains, against modernity's focus on the individual human as its central unit of analysis, that for there to be an individual there must first have been something greater than it, on which it depends. Concomitantly, it insists on the embodied, the creaturely, as the condition of the possibility of epistemology against individualism's prioritisation of rationality. Intersubjectivity is perhaps most easily visible in language, which must be socially instituted in order to have meaning. It is also recognisable in systems that are not reducible to any given individual/s (governmental models, churches, etc.). But intersubjectivity can also describe God: not only in the relations of the Trinity but also in terms of participation (Garrigan, 2004: 198). By recognising their relationships as being dependent on a vast complex of prior relational accomplishments, humans realise that 'The experience of the reality of God is mediated through others' (Peukert, 1986: 274); and 'others', we should add, is not limited to humans.

'Intersubjectivity' is not interaction, a dialogue between two or more subjects; it is a depth-charged communication across time that makes human life viable and mutual understanding possible. As such, it has built into it an 'anamnestic solidarity' with those who have gone before, which brings ethical obligations, particularly in a Christian context. As Peukert describes it, 'faith in the resurrection of Jesus is at once universal solidarity with all others. And as anamnestic solidarity, it is universal solidarity in the horizon of all humanity and of one unified history' (Peukert, 1986: 276). To speak of participation in the life of God thus indicates a *current* mode of belonging, but one that is contingent on intersubjectivity and thereby imbued with the possibility of the transcendent. This removes the accent from *striving* to 'find' or 'make' a home – which assumes one does not have one – to realising the home in which one is already *participating*.

By contrast, Christianity has too often imagined humans' home with God as something that existed before their creaturely birth and something that is to be regained only after their creaturely death. Not only has this idea resulted in abuse of the earth – because earth was seen as mere 'matter' in contrast to God's sacred 'spirit' – but it has also created in human consciousness a pervasive sense of exile. Such a positioning of home *out of this world* produces feelings of separation and longing, and creates the idea that creaturely life is a 'gap' between homes, an interruption in secure belonging – an experience of homelessness, even. In response to this gap, many Christians and Christian-influenced societies have sought home in this life via consumer capitalism and nationalism. How these forces offer apparent anchorage in a time of exile, stifling the longing of unbelonging and easing the pain of separation, will be considered later in this section. First, it is necessary to consider the contours of the underlying distorted Christian conception of home.

1.3 The Gap of the Now

The time before human birth and the promise of eternal life beyond human death have long been imagined as the basis of humans' participation in the life of God. The time in between, however, has been portrayed as a gap in that participation, momentarily and unpredictably interspersed with sustaining grace, which intervenes as if from the same place as the intangible pre-birth or post-death world. For Christians, then, 'this life' has often been understood as a time of disturbance in the history of divine belonging and described in terms of exile from (home in) God. As an early example from the western Church, the last prayer of every day in monastery and chapel alike was the Salve Regina, originating in (at least) the eleventh century:

> Hail, holy Queen, Mother of Mercy,
> Hail our life, our sweetness and our hope.
> To thee do we cry,
> Poor banished children of Eve;
> To thee do we send up our sighs,
> Mourning and weeping in this valley of tears.
>
> Turn then, most gracious advocate,
> Thine eyes of mercy toward us;
> And after this, our exile,
> Show unto us the blessed fruit of thy womb, Jesus [...]

As the prayer makes plain, the nature of being human is understood as 'banishment' to a time and place of 'exile' in which humans sigh, mourn, and weep. It is a description of agony, the profound pain of separation. And it is not an artefact of the agonistic brush with which modern people often paint the early Middle Ages: it remains the final prayer of the Rosary, a popular daily devotional practice in Catholic cultures today.

In the West, Christians have felt exiled because of a theological premise that humans came from God and to God they will return. Jesus, it is claimed, came to make this eventual return possible, so there is some future-derived reassurance: life on earth will be painful, but in death we will go home. The hymn writer Isaac Watts reflects such a theology, while echoing Psalm 90, around 1700:

> Our God, our help in ages past,
> our hope for years to come,
> be thou our guard while troubles last,
> and our eternal home.

Accordingly, whatever the world throws at humans during their short time on earth, their ultimate point of refuge, security, and belonging – their home – is in God, who is elsewhere, in heaven. This modern hymnic expression may be within the reach of cultural memory, but the core mistake goes back a lot further. For example, one of the New Testament apocrypha, *Letter to Diognetus* c.130 CE, says that Christians 'pass their days on earth but have their citizenship in heaven' and they are 'detained in the world as in a prison' (Meecham, 1935: 31). This expresses a subtly, but importantly different, idea to that of Christians being 'in the world but not of the world' (John 17:16), which distinguishes Christ's values and ways from those of the world but does not deny the fundamental appropriateness of creaturely life as the Christian context.

The idea that a Christian's original home is in God, and especially that their future home will be also, helped many people to tolerate suffering in this life: either because of the shift in perspective that comes with seeing the present as nothing compared to an eternal home in God – 'A thousand ages in thy sight are like one evening gone', as Watts sang – or because, as in the Salve Regina, there is the promise of seeing Christ when life is over. And, of course, Diognetus's fellow Christians were being persecuted unto death, and reassurance that life with God lay *ahead* was vitally reassuring.

However, the idea of home as eventual reunion after separation also made Christians vulnerable to a series of destructive projects because, instead of indicating security of belonging with their creator and understanding the present moment as *part of* God's eternal home, it expresses a rupture. For some, like the Psalmist who inspired Watts, the rupture was the product of God's wrath at human sinfulness; for others, it has a more eschatological hue, like those praying the Salve Regina for whom Christ's redemptive work has not yet been fully 'shown'. Either way, it has a long history of inducing insecurity – making humans feel like they do not fully belong with God while they are on earth – and of generating attempts to compensate for it. As brief illustrations, consider these six moments of Christian contemplation of divine belonging:

i. Human time on earth being seen as 'exile' gave rise to the belief that one might accumulate credit in this life, through suffering or sacrifice, to secure one's place in the next. The mediaeval Western church became the mediator of these transactions – through selling indulgences and making salvation conditional on the sacraments – creating a deadly linkage between individual sovereignty and institutional capital. **Belonging became accumulation of capital.**

ii. Reform of the church to 'faith not works' ended clerical mediation of salvation and the practice of buying one's way into heaven, and it brought Christians back to scripture, but it also gave rise in some quarters to the belief that my eternal home with God is a matter for me *primarily as an individual*. God's 'eternal home' became subject to doctrines of predestination, and human community became ordered by emphasis on autonomy and individualism, not collective belonging. Individuals had to be seen to be performing within communities as being 'beyond reproach'. **Belonging became respectability-signalling.**

iii. As Christendom gave way to nation-states, colonisation, and scientific discovery, the idea calcified that eternal home in God was something only for Christians. A dichotomy between Christian and not-Christian became a global organising principle: the West and the Rest. With it came the roots of white supremacy and also the roots of how homelessness is portrayed in the modern world, because there is a pervasive foundational thought-form in Western society that sees some as entitled to belonging/housing and the rest as vagrants, spongers, drop-outs, illegals, losers, and threats – as people experiencing homelessness have been called in my lifetime. **Belonging became entitlement for the superior, who are Christian.**

iv. With industrialisation and colonisation came the loss of the significance of land, of place, to life. This separation matters acutely in and of itself but also, as mentioned in the Introduction, because it so interrupts synapses of belonging that humans' very ability *to relate* is lost. Belonging became defensive – defending property or territory-as-property – and manifested as shape-shifting violence against whatever was rendered as different: slavery in colonial modernity, sectarianism in societies like my own, eco-catastrophe due to first-world extractivist economics, and a normative 'politics of enmity' in today's democracies (Mbembe, 2019). **Belonging became possession and, consequently, racialised,** because the *them* produced by the *us* of the property-defence was ordered, and demeaned, in terms that mapped physiology as use-value.

v. A sense of separation from home-in-God combined in the West with an overemphasis on God as a father-figure: thus, God is imagined as 'head of the household'. When laminated with nationalism's structural thought-form of militant masculinity, the Father of the Nation possesses a sort of authority that is both supreme and heteronormatively male (Du Mez, 2021). Current exponents are easily seen in, for example, Viktor Orbán, Donald Trump, and Vladmir Putin – and in many other previous exemplars, including the Russian Tsars on whom Putin models his image, as well as in less vilified and less visible leaders over the centuries. If God is a white man who is in control of everything, then white patriarchal authority's job is to restore order – and because 'the gap of the now' signals a lost way of ordering the world, order needs to be restored. It is an imperial fantasy that has propped up many a domineering dad at a domestic dinner table as well as being deployed politically in our times to aid a corporate, consumer economy by quelling movements for civil rights, women's rights, immigrant rights, and anti-war voices. **Belonging became the rule of patriarchy.**

vi. The longing for home led to the framing of the nation as home. This was wrought, to some extent, ritually. National anthems and nationalist hymns were (and still are) sung in worship. National colours adorned ecclesial decorations. Worship spaces hosted national flags, sometimes beside the Bible, pulpit, altar, tabernacle, or other authority-point. In Ireland, like other postcolonial places, this meant one sort of flag in one sort of church and another sort of flag in another sort of church: two nationalisms within one territory. Sacramental theology and political theology have a lot to do with one another in this moment, wherein deep longings for belonging seek divine authority not as a pacifist, prophetic, grassroots-organising, social-justice-seeking Christ figure, but as the identity-corralling figure of the nation. **Belonging became alignment with nationalist interests.**

In these six moments, how belonging is understood comes to function theologically as a substitute for the home that is rendered missing by 'the gap of the now'. And yet, in these forms of belonging, human longing for home is only partially and temporarily assuaged. Instead of being assured of their *current* belonging in eternal love and guided in how to access and enjoy it, humans become attached to ultimately unsatisfying objects, and so continue to long for a lost, vital attachment. The gap of the now is thus kept in place, rendering Christians susceptible to ideologies they might otherwise be expected to oppose. Secular citizens of Christian-legacied countries, colonised ones as well as colonising ones, are similarly affected because what is culturally operational is (theology as) a structuring thought-form, not a belief to which one does or does not ascribe. Accordingly, our own era is dominated by the twin forces of nationalism and capitalism, continually evolving the constitutive ideologies of colonial modernity to ease the distress of the gap of the now. Each is afforded quasi-divine glosses, or even elevated to idolatrous extents such that they look like they will supply the divine home for which we long. But they do not. Indeed, they both *cause* homelessness, and deny doing so.

1.4 Minding the Gap: Nationalism and Capitalism

Nationalism is a complex phenomenon, possessing different characteristics in different places at different times and evading any singular definition. Yet one can discern across the globe over the past 200 years a recognisable 'package' of ideas about nation, citizen, and people, and how they 'ought' to interact (Brubaker, 2017). That 'package' expresses the very essence of colonial modernity by ordering both the public sphere and natural resources for optimal control according to the logics of white supremacy. Accordingly, as Gayatri Spivak observes, nationalism is dependent upon both 'the assumptions of ... reproductive heteronormativity' and 'a recoding of [an] underived private as the antonym of the public sphere' – where 'underived private' indicates subaltern life experience (Spivak, 2009: 80). Some believe nationalism has a value beyond this endemic Eurocentrism and male-privileging (e.g., Mylonas and Tudor, 2023), but I share Stephen Backhurst's view that, whatever form it takes, it is an ideology antithetical to the gospel because 'even apparently benign nationalisms rely on quasi-historical myths, selective cultural memories and suspect racial theories, and as such, they undermine human flourishing by prioritising the unstable, abstract notion of "the compatriot" over the concrete reality of "the neighbour"' (Backhurst, 2011: 2). The difficult irony is that nationalism so often does this while speaking the language of Christianity, a religion that (as the following sections will explore) prioritises seeing neighbours *as* compatriots in its scriptural and doctrinal foundations.

Even when nationalism is not explicitly connected to ecclesial spaces as described in the sixth 'belonging' scenario earlier, it nonetheless has significant resonances with Christian thought-forms (and with religion more broadly) (Hastings, 1997). Tracing the origins of modern nationalism to the secularising politics of the nineteenth century, Anthony Smith remarks that nationalism 'substituted the nation for the deity, the citizen body for the church and the political kingdom for the kingdom of God, but in every other respect replicated the forms and qualities of traditional religions' (Smith, 1998: 98). This is not only historically pertinent; contemporary manifestations of supposedly secular nationalisms in Europe and the United States continue similar 'substitutions'. In the United States, for instance, appeals to divine authority to justify nationalist forms of self-organisation range from daily cries of 'God bless America!' in the Capitol's proceedings to the overt claims of white Christian nationalists that currently dominate right-wing politics. According to the latter, the United States is believed to be uniquely called to fulfil God's mission on earth and so needs to be defended against all those who purportedly threaten it – people with the 'wrong' sorts of religion, skin colour, gender, sexuality, and ideas (Perry and Whitehead, 2020). What allows this nationalism to pass as 'Christian' is not only that it is espoused by individuals and lobbies who label themselves Christian, but also the Bible stories it constantly indirectly invokes: the Promised Land, the Second Coming of Jesus and, with echoes of its dreadful use in justifying slavery, the Curse of Ham.

In Europe, it can be tempting to see twenty-first-century US forms of nationalism intertwined with Christian stories and labels as anomalous, but Christian thought-forms undergird nationalist imaginations here too. France's constitutional bolstering of *laïcité* prohibits Islamic religious expression while seeing Christian religious expression as normative. Viktor Orbán's descriptions of the nation along ethno-religious lines, hailing the nation as an 'illiberal Christian democracy' and sidelining the Roma, is even more notable because of the ways Hungary's mainstream (Reformed) Church has authorised these descriptions (Van der Tol, 2024). And in the Netherlands, as Jan Willem Duyvendak observes, the nation is construed as heaven itself: 'a public space where shared "modern" conceptions concerning the "good life" are nourished' – all while racist anti-migration politics flourish

(Duyvendak, 2011: 108–109). The basis of this nation-as-heaven construal is in nostalgia for a (fictional) time when European countries were homogenous, as God allegedly intended them to be.

While in Europe the politics of home manufacture nostalgia for a mythical ancestral past, the US politics of home are rooted in nostalgia for the nuclear family and its much-touted 'values'. The longed-for family is heteronormative: its women are 'homemakers' and its men hold dominant power within the home while working outside it. Nostalgia for this mythical form of home is shot through with resentment at feminism for allegedly killing it (Duyvendak, 2011: 57). Accordingly, US-American home-nostalgia expresses not so much a desire for how actual families might organise themselves in today's world but rather a yearning for what Kirstin Du Mez calls the 'John Wayne virtues', which are: 'masculine strength, aggression and redemptive violence' (Du Mez, 2021: 59). Not concretely realisable (or legal) in most actual households, these yearnings get projected onto the nation, and Christian nationalism sets the nation up as home to establish the 'virtues' for which (some of) the people long.

Framing the nation as home as an outworking of the divine-ordering of the world according to the logics of the white hetero-nuclear family is not confined to the United States. Irish twentieth-century history was similarly structured; independence having been so extensively coded as Roman Catholic family life under clerical control that it is frequently colloquially described as a theocracy – for example, by the esteemed novelist John McGahern (2005): 'By 1950, against the whole spirit of the 1916 Proclamation, the State had become a theocracy in all but name' (279). Furthermore, as Ludger Viefhues-Bailey has exposed, what appears in twenty-first-century Europe as a defence of secular democratic politics is permeated with normatively Christian justifications for sexual and religious regulation. This happens because 'the fearful defense of popular sovereignty – that of the People – animates an obsessive concern over the politics of national reproduction' (2023: 3). Accordingly, in Germany the nation is conceived as symbolically Christian and, because it requires the reproduction of this identity to maintain itself/its security, Islam is framed as anti-nation. (Providing another moment wherein belonging is framed as Christian entitlement, as in **iii** earlier.)

Moreover, combined with the fact that 'Through their representational work, women are on the front lines of delineating the borders of the nation', a situation prevails wherein 'the Muslim woman becomes the collective symbol of what the German nation is not' and conflict ensues about veiling (Viefhues-Bailey, 2023: 77). Similarly in France, women's symbolic status in defining 'home' was at the centre of debates about same-sex marriage. Even as the debates led to legislation permitting it, all sides generally affirmed national identity as normatively heterosexual. 'What was at stake in these debates was the defense of "gender complementarity" and its power to limit the reach of sexual equality, particularly by making sure that women's bodies serve the reproductive needs of the People' (Viefhues-Bailey, 2023: 161) – giving us another moment of framing belonging as patriarchy, as in v earlier. And lest these examples be dismissed as historic, in Ireland in 2024, a proposed constitutional amendment to remove Clause 41:2, which assumes a woman's place is in the home, was roundly rejected in a referendum. When the nation is framed as home, who can belong to it and how they are expected to behave in it is tightly controlled.

Nationalism's power derives from a tacit doctrine of creation, a version of divine/ontological ordering of the world, which enables it to frame the nation as home as simply 'how it's meant to be'. Appealing to nationalism's unspoken theological authority thus legitimates an us/them boundary that would otherwise be questionable. Accordingly, some (us) but not all (them) align themselves with the way God aligned things, and therefore some are entitled to belong/be at home and others are not. Nationalism consequently presents a serious problem because it takes away the equality on which democracy is predicated. As Van der Tol and Gorski explain, 'The sacralisation of nationhood' has 'enabled a programmatic undermining of constitutionalism, and as such poses a threat to the stability political conservatism historically has sought to protect' (2022: 493). A further serious problem is that nationalism embeds homelessness for some into its conception of the nation, *normalising* homelessness for some at the very heart of its definition of itself.

The Christian thought-form that is foundational to all the earlier framings of the nation as home is the gap of the now. Were Christians to feel a full and nourishing sense of being at home in this world, they would not have to manufacture a 'them' to justify their 'us'. Freed from the gap of the now, Christians would feel a sense of belonging, and furnishing a sense of belonging by manufacturing nationalisms would not be needed; indeed, it would be absurd. A similar case may be made regarding capitalism. In modernity, nationalism and capitalism are intrinsically linked: citizens are redefined as consumers, and then as customers (Streeck, 2016). Watching those nightly television programmes about homemaking temporarily fills the gap of the now. So does an Amazon Prime subscription, wearing high-status brand logos on clothing, regularly buying a new car, or addiction to anything that can be bought. The appeal of consumption is rarely ruined by regretting the ecological harm it causes and the global wealth disparity – the poverty – it fosters. Indeed, because the sense of belonging, the home, that is being bought in fetish form ultimately fails to satisfy, we consume yet more.

Capitalism, like nationalism, thus co-opts us into a spurious idea of participation whilst excluding (obviously) 'them' and (insidiously) 'us' from any realisation of what satisfactory participation, real belonging, might mean. Theology's alternative view of belonging as participating in the life of God is made all the more difficult to hear because Christianity has become embroiled in capitalism. As Joerg Rieger points out, many Christians have so thoroughly confused God and Caesar that they are 'worshipping the wrong God' (2018: 1). Capitalism has become so normative that its exploitativeness is invisible to these Christians: 'Unlike the tax collectors and client kings of old, corporate America is generally seen as benevolent or at least innocent' (Rieger, 2018: 116). In such an advanced capitalist system, the original separation – the gap of the now – generates ever-multiplying separations between the gospel of Jesus Christ and the Capitalist Christianity that is the most visible version of 'Christianity' in today's Anglophone world.

If 'the gap of the now' has fostered out-of-control consumption in the West, with associated economic injustices, consider the effects of globalisation in stripping the Global South of its ecologies, assets, and grassroots power. Like a wolf in lamb's clothing, this is not how capitalism advertises itself. Whether in its consumerist, neoliberal, or other protean forms, capitalism is a 'package' that presents itself as helpful, good. The common distinction that capitalism is an economic practice whereas neoliberalism is a philosophy is hard to sustain given the way today's politics, or necropolitics, blur the economic-philosophical distinctions. Neoliberalism relies on economic practices, and nineteenth-century capitalism did not state itself as a philosophy but was evidently based in one. The original object of Marx's critique – a system that allows some to own the means of production without sharing its profits – is still recognisable across the more recent consumerist, globalising, and neoliberal ways it manifests. As Sherry Ortner observes, these shifts in capitalism's terminology merely reflect 'a change in the story or narrative in which [they] are embedded' (Ortner, 2011). The current time of homelessness has to be perceived in this context, inseparable from neoliberalism: the hegemonic domination of capitalism, locally and globally (Harvey, 2005).

The problem with capitalism is not merely that it does not spread its goods equally, but that – again, like nationalism – by entrenching inequalities at all levels, by widening the gap between rich and poor, it undermines democracy (because democracy is predicated on equality) and foments fascism (because fascism is predicated on the power of unregulated elites) (Lane, 2023). However, the problem is also a cycle of homelessness. People are motivated to consume, or to acquiesce to globalised neoliberal practices, because of the sense of participating in something incontrovertible. But the sense of belonging that it promises fails to deliver, and people are left feeling more homeless. In attempting to close the gap of the now via consumption, it is actually expanded, and so greater participation (consumption) is demanded. Even as consumption repeatedly fails to deliver 'belonging', it nonetheless promises a sense of participating in something. That something carries the trace of the divine life in which human participation was designed and from which it has been separated. Eugene McCarraher goes so far as to suggest that: 'Far from being an agent of "disenchantment"', as Weber saw it, capitalism 'has been a regime of enchantment, a repression, displacement, and renaming of our intrinsic and inveterate longing for divinity' (2019: 4). We have, he argues, renamed human participation in the divine life, its belonging there, as a longing for capital and financial security.

The argument in this Element is not that secularisation gave rise to religious *transference* – what William Cavanaugh calls, 'the migration of the holy' (2011). It is that even before capitalism, even before modern nationalism, there was a theological gap widening between humans and God, due to a sense of not being at home, of being far from home, and that gap gave rise to the pain, longing and even terror of unbelonging. It is this state of anxiety, of exile, that allowed nationalism and capitalism to be embraced by Christians, because they provide avatars of 'home'. Moreover, they have increasingly appeared as the only forms of belonging available in this life. To respond, Christians do not need better distribution of the alleged goods of capitalism, nor stronger national borders, nor a nuclear family in a nice house, nor more militaristic masculinity. What they need is to feel that they are actively participating in a life that supplies a deep sense of belonging, one which actually supplies the assurance, security, confidence and peace of home.

Fundamental to both nationalism and capitalism is the practice of defining those who belong by defining those who do not, motivating some to scramble for belonging and causing others to live without it – and allowing no one the rest, peace, and unconcerned security that comes with genuine belonging. A tacit theology of home is at play here but so are actual homes. In Ireland, autonomous home *ownership* is the marker of postcolonial self-realisation and has come to function as symbolically synonymous with citizenship, as it did also in the UK and the US commitment to creating a 'home ownership society' – which helped to cause the 2008 economic crash. This is in part because, as Kathleen Arnold argues, the home that is owned 'both allows for and represents an individual's ability for self-preservation and thus represents the capacity for reason. More broadly, the home is a precondition for citizenship just as the homeland is a precondition for political autonomy and action' (2004: 47). Home ownership thus becomes a materialised form of political nationalism.

Neoliberal capitalism connects synapses at an embodied level between these tropes of the nation as home, the despised other as not part of this home, and individual legitimation as citizens accomplished through home ownership. It does this through myriad cultural phenomena, including all those television programmes on home-improvement (you cannot knock down an internal wall or paint an external one bright green if you live in a rented property), and in many countries, you cannot vote if you are homeless. Neoliberalism also knits together these realities through the limits and burdens inflicted by debt; most people nowadays must take on vast debt to purchase, furnish, maintain, or inhabit a home – debt which benefits global liquidity markets that then turn localities into 'developments' no locals can afford (Aalbers, 2012).

Capitalist manipulations mean that home now functions as an institution of the modern mind: a complex, fundamental ordering principle. Home is my own domain, to which I am entitled, the occupation of which signals my legitimacy and belonging. My own four walls are not just my home, but not-home to specific others. What Benedict Anderson once said of the nation can now be said of the home: it is 'an imagined political community – and imagined as both inherently limited and sovereign' (2006: 6). As such, even the intimacies of our lifeworld – *haim*, the etymological root of 'home' – have been colonised by a globalising capitalist ethic and our homes have taken on the status, affect, and political clout of institutions. What they institute, or rather what our idea of home institutes, over and over, is separation. Home is a bulwark against what we would reject, a site of consumption and retreat and of (dubious) safety. But these separations – us and them, insiders and outsiders – fail to fill the gap of the now; indeed, they reproduce it.

1.5 Participation in the Life of God *as Home*

The 'the gap of the now' is a theological mistake, based not in biblical traditions but in exploitative ones. When Psalm 90 speaks of God as eternal, and Genesis 3:19 says, 'You are dust and to dust you will return', and 2 Cor 5:1 says, 'For we know that if the earthly tent we live in is destroyed, we have a building from God, a house not made with hands, eternal in the heavens', they are affirming human *belonging* in God's creation rather than human abandonment therein. The pain of perceived abandonment that has propelled humans to seek pain-relief, and the insecurity of unbelonging which has created a state of defensiveness, are not what the biblical vision of home sets out. The biblical vision is one of participation in the life of God during our earthly as well as eternal lives. The problem with this is that participation in the life of God as a theology of home is potentially an overly abstract proposition, an ancient assertion that doesn't

A Theology of Home in a Time of Homelessness   23

connect with today's lived realities. I therefore seek to concretise it in the following sections via three biblically based constitutive elements: discipleship as home, companionship as home, and sacramentality as home.

2 Discipleship

Peter reveals the sense of insecurity seemingly induced by discipleship when he exclaims, 'Look, we've left everything and followed you. What then will we have?' But Jesus replies with an assurance of abundant and varied forms of security: 'everyone who has left houses or brothers or sisters or fathers or mother or children or fields, for my name's sake, will receive a hundredfold, and will inherit eternal life' (Matt 19:27–29). Significantly, given 'the gap of the now' identified in the previous section, the almost identical saying in Mark (10:29–30) specifies that the promised bounty will be received 'now in this age' as well as in the age to come. In these and similar sayings, Jesus exhorts his followers to adopt, and reassures them about the rewards of, a way of life that eschews contemporary cultural expectations for home and family. To the rich young man who asks how to enter eternal life (Matt 19:21), Jesus says, 'sell your possessions, give the money to the poor, follow me'. And in Luke 14:33, he makes even plainer what 'following' requires, regardless of one's wealth: 'none of you can become my disciple if you do not give up all your possessions'.

Yet the life Jesus actually led indicates that he did not mean for his followers to live with no points of continuity or connection, because he relied upon and obviously valued these things in his own life. He returned over and over to the same friends' houses in Bethany – Peter's mother-in-law's house, Lazarus's house – and from the cross he ensures a home for his mother with his beloved disciple (John 19:27). What then did he mean by his repeated eschewal of home in calls to discipleship? As the aforementioned references demonstrate, it is part of a wider eschewal of possession. It is homes as possessions, as things that hold one back, that must be left; homes that are facilitators of the circuitry of discipleship are needed. Jesus does not merely say, 'renounce your possessions'; he issues the rejoinder to 'follow me'. And so we can discern a pattern: discipleship replaces possessing and, as this section will suggest, can itself constitute 'home', because to follow Jesus is to participate in the life of God, now.

2.1 New Testament Discipleship

There are many references to following (*akolouthein/akolouthountes*) in the New Testament, and they are used in various ways, as one would expect given the diversity of the audiences for whom its books were written. The word 'followers' can thus be found referring to the crowds receiving Jesus, or to individually called or acknowledged disciples (a category equally applicable to women and men) (Schüssler Fiorenza, 1993), or to the 'armies of heaven' in the Book of Revelation. The Gospels and Acts use the word 'disciple' (*mathētēs*) interchangeably with 'follower', but the other New Testament texts do not always do so. Indeed, Paul does not use the Greek word for disciple at all and the Synoptics often indicate a specifically teacher-student type of relationship when they deploy *mathētēs*. Yet all these different usages of the terms for following and discipleship in the New Testament contain what Richard Longenecker discerns as 'patterns' of Christic and ecclesial imagination, amounting to a common kernel of 'Christian self-understanding and practice' that transcends the temporal and ideological variations in which it is contextually described (1996: 5).

Significantly, Longenecker notes that 'Those of the Way' is how the earliest Christians referred to themselves (1996: 1). The Way is what was revealed in Jesus Christ and it is centred on him – 'I am the Way, the Truth and the Life' (John 14:6) – but it is vital to any theological interpretation of the Way to note from the outset that it is not understandable as the story of one person alone. Mary bore the Way, John the Baptist prepared it, and Jesus's disciples followed it. For two millennia, Christians have been baptised into this same Way – at Jesus's invitation, by the power of the Spirit, and with plentiful role models in discipleship for how to live it. These include Mary Magdalene, Mary of Bethany, the Samaritan woman, the apostles, and all those unnamed biblical characters who encountered Jesus and were emancipated by their faith in him. It is a distinct Way, different to others – hence the capitalised first letter. As Shawn Copeland remarks: 'To follow the "Way" [Jesus] teaches requires that his disciples take up a new and different "way" of being *in* and *for* the world' (2018: 107). Given that this Way is specifically that of Christ, the incarnation, it might reasonably be interpreted as *part of* the life of God, and not merely indicative of it. Following the Way can then be seen as participation in that life, and the Logos mode of dwelling becomes home in the world.

Too often, though, Jesus's Way has been characterised as a 'homeless' way. Accordingly, verses such as Luke 9:58 and Matt 8:20, 'Foxes have holes, and birds of the air have nests; but the Son of Man has nowhere to lay his head' are prone to be interpreted as a sacralisation of rootlessness. Even Rosemary Radford Ruether describes the prophet Jesus as 'a homeless wanderer in the present system of society' (1993: 122). But Jesus's way of life was, in fact, an acceptable and not marginal first-century mode of life: a symbiotic relationship between itinerant charismatics and the supportive settled communities they moved between (Theissen, 1978). Moreover, when Jesus's lifestyle is interpreted as 'homeless', divine life itself is idealised as homeless, resulting in the perils, pain, isolation, and injustice of actual homelessness being minimised (Sennett, 1990: 6). Such an interpretation also results in a weakened or even distorted understanding of the complex realities of discipleship: the gospel calls people to follow Jesus not into destitution and suffering but into inter-connected forms of human life (like the mutuality between itinerants and settled communities in first-century Palestine). While the forms of life, the ways of dwelling, that Jesus modelled and called for may not rely on possession, they are nothing like the forms of homelessness, material or existential, described in the Introduction.

While Jesus may neither have decried homes *per se*, nor himself been 'homeless', the discipleship to which he called people was nonetheless predicated on a disposition of radical vulnerability. To forgo home and family, abandon one's fields or fishing boat or, if rich, sell all one's possessions and give the money to the poor was as demanding then as it is now. This is because 'Those of the Way' were/are required not merely to follow, but to *take up the cross* and follow (Mark 8:34–36; Matt 16:24; Luke 9:23, 24a). Following necessitates living, as Copeland puts it, 'at the disposal of the cross' (2018: 105) because 'the Way' is the way *of Jesus*, and Jesus's way – God's way to new life – was through the cross. This is challenging. Taking up the cross does not necessitate repeating the trial, torture, and violent death suffered by Christ (although it has involved this for some); it means sacrificing a life grounded by possessions for what, in worldly terms, seems a precarious and uncertain life. As Sallie McFague explains, 'the way' *is* the cross, and the cross is 'dying to one's own life, trying to live a new, self-sacrificing love' (2021: 3–4). It is precisely in the eschewing of possession that one takes up the cross. By doing so, one aligns with Christ's refusal of the normative but death-dealing ethic of possessing, and discovers a new way of living.

The cross is about eschewing possession because possessing is about power: specifically, top-down power, having power-over. Possessing is at the root of both capitalist and nationalist responses to 'the gap of the now' discussed in the previous section not because having (stuff, identifications) distracts us, nor even because it roots us, but, rather, because the having gives us a sense of power when we might otherwise be feeling separated and apparently powerless. It is, however, a death-dealing sort of power, endlessly reproducing the logic of othering: polluting the earth, exploiting and killing people, deadening our own spirits. In its later books, including Acts, the New Testament gives plentiful testimony to the fulfilment of Jesus's promise that difficult though the way of the cross may be, it is rewarding: 'followers were transformed by the knowledge of Christ that they entered into through their engagement in, and then continuation of, his ministry' (Ward, 2009: 277).

Of particular help in understanding how following the way of the cross is a rewarding strategy despite all the renunciation involved is the theological concept of divine kenosis: the idea that God self-emptied God's love, through Christ's cross, into the world, ushering in a new phase in the work of creation and redemption by the Holy Spirit. The self-emptying service demanded of those who would follow Jesus is, then, both initiated and fuelled by the self-emptying love of God, in Christ, on the cross. As John Donahue explains: 'To share in his power is not to possess power of prestige and playing lord over others, but is to practice the self-emptying service which becomes the source of liberation to the many (Mark 10:41–45)' (Donahue, 1978: 386). Kenosis is the key to understanding the power of Christian discipleship precisely because it is – perhaps paradoxically – both an evacuation of worldly markers of power and, instead, a participation in vulnerability (even unto death) as the locus of divine love. However, in positioning kenosis as key, it is vital to heed the insights of feminist theologians who note the habitually gendered ways Christianity interpreted self-giving and self-sacrificing (Mercedes, 2022); otherwise we replicate a view of home in which men thrive at women's expense.

2.2 Discipleship as Politics

Kenosis is, then, perhaps best understood through current political questions, because Christian discipleship in our time can never not be political (Ward, 2009) and because concretising the existential in terms of the political avoids the dangers of abstraction Mercedes (and others) warn against. Amplifying the importance of kenosis in relation to the current climate crisis, McFague asks: 'What if we really opened our minds and hearts to a very different worldview that suggests a type of power that our society sees as wrong, ineffective and maybe even foolish?' (2021: 9). The climate crisis and homelessness are linked, not only through the many 'climate refugees' being created, but also at the level of theology: to follow Jesus/the Way in relation to climate catastrophe demands a self-emptying stance that can feel like a recipe for precarity and social exclusion, and represents a stark contrast to the seeming security and social acceptability afforded by possessing stuff, property, people, enterprises, relationships or fixed identities. It also involves adopting a life of following, what Copeland calls a 'lived mystical-political way' (2018: 110), and trusting it *as* home. It is in these ways that Christian discipleship gives rise to a politics of 'following' instead of 'possessing', and relinquishing what one possesses is essential to being able to follow. Indeed, one cannot do one without the other (Luke 14:33). But how?

In his *Theology of the Built Environment*, Tim Gorringe suggests that human habitations are aligned with God's purpose only when they are set in the service of 'politics' and not of property or possession, meaning politics and possession must be decoupled. He remarks that, fundamentally, 'theology has overlooked the fact that politics is about possession. This is extraordinary given founding narratives about conquest and promised land' (2002: 27). And he argues, based on the Hebrew Bible, that land, being created, belongs to God, who created it, and thus for humans it is encountered entirely by grace: it is gift, not possession. Taken seriously, such a view literally takes the ground from under the feet of property speculators. Land was given by God, Gorringe argues from the doctrine of creation, to be held in common, not sequestered and traded as a commodity that benefits only a few. In doing so, he recalls earlier Christians, such as Gerrard Winstanley in seventeenth-century Britain, whose goal was to 'make the earth a common treasury for all, both rich and poor' (Gorringe, 2002: 67). The movement of which he was a leader, the Diggers, posed such a significant threat to the dominant socio-economic system, which was based in property ownership, that it was brutally put down.

Similar movements today struggle to arrive at an idea of land or the built environment as anything other than property, because the forces that have created modernity as a time of homelessness have made them seem 'naturally' so. Nationalism does this, capitalism does this, and the ideology that undergirds all their shape-shifting forms is whiteness. Not only does this underlying and unspoken force produce environmental racism – examples of which include the situating of waste-treatment or other toxin-producing industries adjacent to Black neighbourhoods in the United States, locating Travellers' halting sites by motorway junctions in Ireland, or scheming to evacuate UK immigrants to Rwanda – it also goes much further affecting every aspect of modernity's organisation of land for habitation or production or both. As Jennings puts it: 'Whiteness is a way of materialising one's desire to order the world through buildings, bodies, and design at the horrific cost to peoples', which becomes difficult to detect or oppose because 'Whiteness roots a master-slave dialectic into the ground itself' (2023). Thus, conceptual structures of entitlement and exclusion seem to arise from the habitable environment, obscuring the truth that private gain and top-down power were first relentlessly imposed upon it, and continue to be.

Divine might is commonly but distortedly associated with these worldly power-brokers rather than with the way of the cross, and the God of Israel and of Jesus is forgotten or even co-opted as perverse justification for them – as when so many missionaries supported European colonisation on the grounds that it was saving the souls of the indigenous peoples. Christian theology should be at odds with such distortions because, as Gorringe says, 'setting limits to absolute possession, and bringing it under proper democratic control, is a political realisation of belief in God as Creator' (2002: 77). It is also fundamental to the politics of discipleship outlined earlier. What Christ calls his disciples to follow involves an idea of home *as a specific mode of dwelling*, one that helps to furnish a theology of home capable of challenging cultural norms of property and possession.

To help get round the ways that home is intrinsically understood as 'property' in the West, as 'possession' – whether as an earth that can be exploited, or as a developer's portfolio for 'making a killing', or as a house for a nuclear family – it might be helpful to regard 'discipleship as politics' as such *a mode of dwelling*. To this end, the remainder of this section will ask what it is to dwell, informed by two very different texts: Heidegger's essay 'Building, Dwelling, Thinking', written in the context of the post-war housing crisis in Europe, and John 1:14.

2.3 Dwelling – Heidegger

Heidegger's Nazi views in other essays are deplorable, and symptomatic of just how dangerous the distorted views of belonging described in Section 1 can be; nonetheless, his 1951 essay insisted, against the grain, on the primacy of 'dwelling' to the human condition at another time of extensive homelessness in Europe. It did so by arguing that dwelling consists of being in one's world as in a *heimat* – a whole, holistic lifeworld – and I will mine his proposal for two insights.

The first insight is that to dwell is essentially to belong, and belonging is both multifaceted and inherently inter subjective. Heidegger articulates a distinction between residing and dwelling. Everyone resides somewhere, even if it is a refugee camp or a cardboard box in the bus station; but humans are creatures that fundamentally, as a condition of their very being, desire to belong and are dissatisfied by merely residing. The two problems this helps a theology of home to face are that, in eschewing possession, a view of home as residing will not work because it does not afford the belonging that humans need. And belonging to a singular entity, such as a house or a nation, is not adequate for an experience of dwelling, because dwelling exists only in relation to the 'fourfold' – earth, sky, divinities, and mortals (1971: 149 [1951]). (Somewhat like the Trinity, the fourfold is a unity of a discernible number of intrinsic and related aspects.) Human belonging, Heidegger thought, had been too long aligned with these four aspects in atomised, separate forms, resulting in multiple forms of failure to belong. Heidegger argued that adopting an integrative approach restored humanity to a sense of belonging *in the world*. This he termed *Mitsein*, 'being-with' – in other words, letting each aspect be discernible as what it is in essence but doing so by seeing it as connected to the other three.

There is much that could be said of this theory, but what matters for this Element are both its force as a model for intersubjectivity as the key to an adequate sense of belonging for humans, and the ways that, when applied to Christian discipleship, it draws attention to the essential and complex inter-relationality of the task. Such radical intersubjectivity is a foil to the mistake identified in Section 1 as 'belonging as respectability-signalling' because it proves false any claims to an individual's power to alone secure their own belonging. The project of modernity has had at its philosophical and political centre, and as the unit of any discursive analysis, the individual. To reconceive the individual as inseparable from the fourfold, to insist that the human instinct to belong can only be satisfied that way, is to radically alter how human nature – and its intrinsic need for dwelling – is understood. Heidegger's articulation of multifaceted (fourfold) belonging as the means of dwelling creates an insistence on an intersubjective view of being human which can allow the message of the gospel to be better understood.

Intersubjectivity is at the very core of the gospel. As noted earlier, the Way is not the route of a lone actor. Jesus's own itinerant lifestyle was a symbiotic one within his context, and the mode of dwelling to which he called his disciples was one based on life with him, and with each other, but not on possessions. However, the intersubjectivity of discipleship does not consist simply of being in relationship with whoever happens to be around. Christ's disciples are to be found (only) among people experiencing specific conditions. As Rowan Williams remarks, discipleship 'means being in the company of the people whose company Jesus seeks and keeps. ... the excluded, the disreputable, the wretched, the self-hating, the poor, the diseased ... if your discipleship is not intermittent but a way of being, you will find yourself in the same sort of company as he is in' (2016: 11). The politics of discipleship arises from the orientation, dispositions, sensibilities, and commitments to which such a mode of dwelling gives rise.

The second insight Heidegger's essay offers this Element is the fact that dwelling is wrought. As he says, 'We do not dwell because we have built, but we build and have built because we dwell, that is, because we are dwellers' (1971: 148). Accordingly, dwelling does not happen without building. Building in this sense is not only a matter of erecting bricks and mortar; it is the ongoing, holistic, and 'poetic' work of inhabiting the fourfold. Reflecting on the shared etymological root of the words for dwelling and being, Heidegger writes: 'The way in which you are and I am, the manner in which we humans are on the earth, is *Buan*, dwelling ... The old word *bauen*, which says that man *is* insofar as he *dwells*, this word *bauen*, however also means at the same time to cherish and to protect, to preserve and to care for, specifically to till the soil, to cultivate the vine' (1971: 147). 'Building' consists of these necessary actions. There is a productive analogy here for understanding discipleship as participation in the life of God. After baptism, people may call themselves Christians, but 'to be' Christian, to be a disciple, involves a very specific set of behaviours. As Copeland remarks, 'A praxis of compassionate solidarity, justice-love, and care for the poor and oppressed is a sign that we are on the "way" Jesus is' (2018: 123).

Dwelling for Christians is wrought by following Jesus, by being of the Way, meaning it is wrought not merely through baptism but through discipleship. This happens not by assent or association but by divesting one's possessions, practising non-violence, bearing prophetic witness/challenging misuses of power, living among 'the least of these', not accumulating personal wealth, forgiving (seven times seventy times), praying, loving God, and loving one's neighbour, and considering the stranger in your midst as a neighbour – so unappealing and difficult a task that it deserves its own discussion, which follows in the next section.

Following Jesus in these ways can become the substance of participation in the life of God. As such, it frames 'home' as *a way of being in the world* and not something that can be bought. As Amy Plantinga Pauw puts it, 'Being Christ's disciples is less a matter of claiming secure possessions than of being a centrifugal force of God's love in the world' (2017: 30). Early Christian testimony suggests this Way was, and can yet be, home for the Christian, as a way of belonging, and as a way of building:

> All who believed were together and had all things in common; they would sell their possessions and goods and distribute the proceeds to all, as any had need. Day by day, as they spent much time together in the temple, they broke bread at home and ate their food with glad and generous hearts, praising God and having the goodwill of all the people. (2 Acts: 44–47)

To return to the name that early Christians called themselves: 'Those of the Way' is a telling phrase. 'Of' is genitive grammatically; it denotes belonging-to. The disciples are not said to be 'on' the Way, as a way might typically be engaged. So it is far from new to imagine discipleship *as* belonging (to the Way) and, accordingly, as participating in the life of God.

One final point to observe in Heidegger's attempt to reframe dwelling as both wrought and sufficiently intersubjective to afford deep belonging is to note that he does so through active verbs: building, thinking, dwelling. In the Conclusion, I will develop this observation to suggest the theological usefulness of reconceiving home as a verb instead of a noun; but here we need to consider a little further what is meant theologically by 'dwelling'.

2.4 Dwelling – John 1:14

'The word was made flesh and dwelt among us.' The verb for dwelling used in this verse is *eskēnōsen*, tent pitching. For today's readers, by imaging the divine as having been born into the world in human form, opting for a tent rather than a palace, John's Gospel sets from its outset a pattern of noting both the proximity/closeness and non-possession-oriented character of divine incarnation. But it would have had other, specific connotations for John's Jewish readers/listeners that are still salient today. Tent pitching was how ancient Israelites were commanded to create the *mishkan* – the residence – for God by Moses (which became known in Latin as *tabernāculum* and in English as tabernacle). Much later, the tabernacle would be solidified as the Temple (957 BCE), but for the generations of wandering ancient Hebrews, a tent that could be pitched wherever they had to move to was their assurance of God's faithfulness to the covenant God had made with Israel. Many New Testament scholars have noted the resonances in John's prologue of the Tabernacle Narrative (Exodus 25–31, 35–40), but this particular verse, with its key verb of tent pitching, carries an additional meaning. In Exodus 25:8–9, Israel is told to pitch a tent so that God can dwell among his people, and so in John 1:1–14, as Raymond Brown notes, 'we are being told that the flesh of Jesus Christ is the new localization of God's presence on earth, and that Jesus is the replacement of the ancient Tabernacle' (1966: 33). To avoid supersessionism, we might amend Brown's commentary to: Jesus is the expansion of the ancient Tabernacle.

The way this verse connects the verb *eskēnōsen* to the Logos – the animating, authorial principle of creation – is a deliberate antidote to possession-thinking because it establishes a contingent and dynamic, rather than a fixed and static, meaning for the way Jesus dwelt on earth. It is a combination that, to its original hearers, would have indicated God's desire to dwell with God's people – it was God's mode of covenant enactment – assuring them that God is not up in the sky, or in a golden calf, but is with God's creation, dwelling amid God's people, now.

A further echo would also have been audible in this verse to John's community: God's work in creation. Gary Anderson traces an arc across the Hebrew Bible from creation to tabernacle (and to temple) through specific repeated vocabulary and textual patterns such that 'When God indwells the Tabernacle, the goal of the created order has been reached ... creation reaches completion with the indwelling of the deity' (2023: 34). He sees this repeated (in pacing as well as vocabulary) in John's Prologue, such that readers hear the echoes of Genesis in addition to the Tabernacle Narratives and can conclude that 'the world was created ... for the purpose of revealing the glory of the Word' (2023: 35). To follow in Christ's mode of dwelling, then, is not merely to live contingently, it is to connect at the level of creation and to participate in the fulfilment of creation's purpose.

Rather than being rooted in possession, this mode of dwelling is responsive, embedded in community, and intrinsically connected to ancestral histories. One might speak, then, of discipleship not just as a mode of dwelling but as 'a Logos mode of dwelling', meaning that it is fundamentally creative – in the dual sense of rooted in the Spirit's work in Creation and in our current, Spirit-led, contingent, improvisational efforts at following Christ. How does this notion of a dwelling place relate to the theological idea of home? For God, the tent is not home – it is merely a residence. Creation and covenant are the home, and they continue through the Logos that once dwelt in a person and now dwells in those that follow him.

2.5 Homing in on Home

Just as following Jesus – discipleship – is a matter of continuous flux and creative responsiveness, so the idea of home changes accordingly; it is a way of being that evolves over time. Following Christ involves a radical sense of commitment to 'being' that is constituted by inhabiting the now, moving with it, rather than experiencing it as a gap. By focusing on *following*, 'home' is rendered a non-static thing. Thus, when Jesus said, 'follow me', he wasn't saying 'abandon all housing'; he was saying: 'don't let possessions prevent you from living the gospel. Attachment to these limited structures of association, alignment and alliance is what enables occupying imperial forces to colonise your minds as well as your material and economic resources, making impossible God's purpose for you, individually and collectively.'

Crucial to this view is that what is being followed is Christ, not a given path, rulebook, catechism, handbook, or route map but, instead, a living person. As Ward notes, 'Jesus instructs Simon and his brother Andrew to "follow *me*," not simply to follow his teaching' (2009: 276). Heidegger's essay helps draw out the implications of this remark for how theology might reconceptualise 'home', by directing us to the anti-modernist hermeneutic of intersubjectivity. Thus, before being given a single thing to 'do' or a single teaching to heed, Jesus calls disciples, primarily, into relationship. Donahue puts it even more plainly: 'His mission in the world is not one of an isolated prophet, but involves the engagement of others called out of the ordinary way to follow his way. He does not exist except in community with others' (Donahue, 1978: 386).

What is it then to follow Christ as home? It is to be in relationship with Christ, others, and all of creation as an extension of the divine Logos's creating force in the world. It is to follow Christ in the sense of patterning one's life on what

Christ did, which was to dwell within the creaturely world, participating in the life of God as a human enmeshed in the same intersubjective conditionality of all creatures. As McFague remarks, 'Trinitarian Christianity and nature share a common characteristic – intrinsic relationality' (McFague, 2021: xi). But it is to do so in a specific mode, not by slavishly following rules but by inhabiting the intersubjectivity that discipleship instantiates with Christ. Christ did not 'dwell among us' as some alien creature, with a special tent; Christ did so as a human, and thereby showed humans the relational possibilities of *being* human. Christ, 'dwelling among us', is what enables our discipleship, and thus our ability to participate in the life of God.

3 Companionship

As the previous section observed, a theological understanding of 'home' has to be rooted in God's express desire to dwell among God's people – as (ongoing) Creator, covenant-maker, and Christ. That section explored 'following Christ' as a crucial route whereby Christians can participate in the life of God because it allows them simultaneously to inhabit and realise this dwelling of God in creation and so to reconceptualise their sense of what 'home' means. John's Gospel in particular emphasises the *symbiotic* character of such a route. Humans follow Jesus, in whom God dwells, and through their discipleship they participate in the life of God. John's Gospel describes this as God coming to dwell in those followers: 'Those who love me will keep my word, and my Father will love them, and we will come to them and make our home with them' (John 14:23). This verse has often been interpreted in a spiritual sense: the divine Father and Son will come and make their home in human *hearts*. But what if it were interpreted materially, as suggesting that God might come and actually make God's home with those who follow Christ?

In Ireland, such a shift in theological emphasis might appeal. It reinforces popular identification with, and tourist-industry touting of, the idea of our country as a place of *céad míle fáilte* – a hundred thousand welcomes. It also echoes the persistent folk practice of placing a lit candle in one's front window on Christmas Eve, to indicate a welcome for the Christ child who, it is thought, wanders the world on that night, looking for a home. But the reality of adding over 100,000 Ukrainians into a country of 5 million people within 18 months has been educative – producing the rapid growth of a far-right political movement and violent protesters not previously prominent in Ireland. The Christ child coming to make his home with you on Christmas night sounds lovely, but the reality of God in human form seeking a home with those who follow Christ is far from romantic. It is disruptive, and it challenges human constructs of belonging, especially so when 'native' people are lacking housing (and other services, such as health care) and newcomers are prioritised in the allocation of resources.

In response to this scenario, this section considers biblical teaching about the *dynamics* of an outsider arriving into a space others consider to be their home, especially when the outsider is seen as some sort of threat to, for instance, access to resources, community cohesion, or identity. This teaching comes in the form of repeated injunctions to love those you would prefer not to love – which will be considered next – as well as in certain parables, such as Luke 15:11–32, where a faithful son is hurt and angry that his father would throw a banquet for the return of a squandering son who left, when he had been 'at home' all the time and a banquet had never been thrown for him.

3.1 Celebrate Life

This story is often interpreted in such a way that God is the father, loving his son despite the great pain and shame he has caused him, but I would like to consider what might be learned about the dynamics of sharing housing with those with whom we would prefer not to share housing if God/Christ is interpreted as the prodigal son. This reorientates the Christian's role to that of the father figure: going out to meet those who show up, often in unexpected form. The parable hinges on the father's reply to the younger son's complaint: 'We had to celebrate and rejoice, because this brother of yours was dead and *has come to life*; he was lost and has been found.' The Christic echoes of dying but coming back to life support the interpretation of God *as* the prodigal. I suggest that reading the parable such that God *is* the lost one, might alter the prevailing, mistaken theology of home outlined in Section 1. Because to claim that, no matter what, life itself is to be celebrated is both to root theology in life, now, and to insist that the bonds between the living, *qua* life, far outweigh the boundaries that arise between them.

Such an interpretation holds that the circumstances that lead one individual or group to understand another as 'other' – less deserving, or even effectively dead, as in the parable – can be altered by remembering that life, all life, is to be rejoiced in, rather than socially ordered according to the logic of top-down power: all life is divine. Dispositions of with-ness and of co-identifying overcome othering, and can be cultivated, as in the parable, by remembering that humans are most bonded not by family ties (which can break), but by life itself, by being alive. Life is something to notice and celebrate, and prioritising such a disposition has a certain amount of power to counter cultures habitually ordered by distinctions of who is deserving and who is not.

But as the figure of the younger son in the parable reminds us, God making God's home in material as well as cardiac spaces can be very difficult. Even if, in the heat of the moment, one can be persuaded to celebrate life, it does not necessarily lead to getting along. As another parable makes clear, God dwelling – materially – amid God's people means people are faced, over and over, with the challenge of accepting people who are not ordinarily acceptable. Luke 10:29–37, the so-called parable of the Good Samaritan, relies for its key challenge – 'Who is my neighbour?' – on a strong common consensus about who was normatively despised or accepted. In Jewish lore, the triad of Priest and Levite was completed by Israelite; to replace Israelite with Samaritan was shocking because Samaritans were so reviled, so other. The 'select exclusions' involved in modernity's conceptualisation of home are as calcified as the ancient Near Eastern exclusions that Jesus challenged, even as colonial modernity produces gendered, raced and classed 'others' differently. But the parable's meaning also relies on knowledge of the Hebrew Bible's much repeated command to care for strangers, and that, too, can illuminate a way of participating in the life of God today.

3.2 Care for Strangers

The books of the Hebrew Bible were written in contexts in which displacement was common and so, therefore, were strangers. The impetus for the settled community to close the door, protect turf, or (metaphorically) to pull up the drawbridge was as strong then as it is in the rampant anti-immigrant attitudes that dominate politics today. Indeed, so commonplace was the experience of displacement that the Torah's repeated injunction to treat the stranger well is often premised on the fact that the Israelites were treated badly during their own exile from home: 'You shall not oppress a resident alien; you know the heart of an alien, for you were aliens in the land of Egypt' (Exodus 23:9). Or, after stating that God loves the strangers, 'You shall also love the stranger, for you were strangers in the land of Egypt' (Deuteronomy 10:19). Moreover, the Hebrew Bible spells out that this is not a matter of tolerating strangers by affording them a second-class status, but instead of endowing them with full civic belonging: 'The alien who resides with you *shall be to you as the citizen among you*; you shall love the alien as yourself, for you were aliens in the land of Egypt' (Lev 19:34).

This rationale has strong resonances with current progressive rhetoric in Ireland, which makes the following appeal: the Irish have often been migrants across the world, fleeing persecution and extreme poverty, and it was very difficult to be in that position, so Ireland ought now to welcome migrants.

The modern version is an argument that swiftly moves from empathy to charity: given that one knows how painful something is, one will not inflict it on others. But this is not a strong enough argument to combat the anti-immigration movements because unlike the Jewish version, with its premise in the security of a covenant between God and Israel, it is not predicated on a theologically sound idea of home, and the alternative functional nationalist, capitalist idea of home is a significant reason why migrants are not welcomed. First, there is a housing crisis and if the state allocates housing to immigrants but not to citizens it causes not only resentment but also existential fears, fears that are based in both economics (scarcity of resources leads to unaffordable prices) and in the post-colonial memory of the trauma of being denied a home in one's own country. Second, many people arriving in Ireland today, and on the climate-driven horizon, are seeking to make a new home, not to take temporary shelter, and so their otherness – cultural, religious, linguistic, and aesthetic – can feel like a threat to the supposed security of Irish identity. There is a fear that such an influx will destabilise the national identity, the cultural 'home'. Why, then, should we love the alien as ourselves?

The answer to this question is that, as the New Testament suggests, the possibility of experiencing a deep sense of belonging during one's lifetime, and of fullness of relationship with the divine (and thus of 'home') depends on one's love for strangers; and not just amenable strangers but also enemy strangers. The question, then, becomes one not so much of why we should afford a welcome to the stranger but of how we might do so?

The word for stranger in the Hebrew Bible (*gēr*) can refer to a variety of individuals and groups. Translated alien, resident-alien, foreigner, or sojourner, as well as stranger, it usually – though not always – denotes a temporary status. But *Gērīm* can also be called *nokhrī* or *zār*, carrying the connotation of 'enemy'. Wil Gafney discerns a distinction in how these words are used that offers an insight to this question of the *dynamics* of caring for strangers. Noting how Deuteronomy demands hospitality towards one sort of outsider while maintaining others as enemies who can be vilified or even exterminated, she asks, 'what is the difference between a sojourning stranger and an enemy stranger?' She deduces that it is 'one relationship at a time', meaning that *Gerīm* become the sort of strangers who are to be cared for, instead of the sort of strangers who are to be feared or despised, when they are interacted with as neighbours. She notes that 'Kings tells us that even an Amalekite was a sojourner in Israel in the time of David and Saul, serving in the Israelite army (2 Sam:1–13). And the Amalekites were the most despised of enemy nations … with regular calls in the Torah for their annihilation' (Gafney, 2011).

Another example might be taken from the Book of Ruth and its story of the transformation of foreigner-enemies to foreigner-beloveds through the relationship of Ruth and her mother-in-law Naomi. As Gafney remarks, 'When no one knows any of "them" it is easy to believe every horror story and consent to the most inhumane practices in the name of self-preservation. But when one person knows another person from the outsider-stranger community then it's no longer possible to talk about all of them as a collective' (Gafney, 2011). Moreover, there is a profound tradition in the Hebrew Bible of God turning up in the form of a stranger, such as the three strangers who meet Abraham and Sarah in the desert or the man with whom Jacob wrestles all night long. This tradition gave rise to the teaching of Hebrews 13:2: 'Do not neglect to show hospitality to strangers, for by doing that some have entertained angels without knowing it.' Of course, the problem is that a stranger feels like *a stranger* at the point they are encountered and, as in the Bible stories, they are only revealed to have been divine/Godly after they have left; hence the commands to love strangers, to encourage a hospitable choice in the face of real, felt uncertainty. The risk that they will turn out to be an enemy is the risk one is commanded to take; and if they do, Christians are commanded to love them just the same.

3.3 Love Your Enemies

Despite the prevalence of biblical injunctions to love one's enemies, there has hardly been a generation of Christians that has not found it very difficult, or even impossible, to put them into practice. Christian history – from its earliest days in Rome, when the non-Jewish Christians did not want to reintegrate Jews returning after the death of Claudius (Romans 2–4, 9–11, 14), to the horrors of the Nazi Holocaust, and to today's white Christian nationalism – demonstrates the strength of the contrary impulse to avoid, despise, discriminate against, and even kill the supposed other. My own context is one in which Christians have often violently separated themselves from each other: Protestant vs. Catholic. And while the recent peace in the British-Irish relationship is a huge achievement, given the extent of animosity in our history, this lack of love for neighbour is far from safely in the rear-view mirror: both housing and schooling in Belfast today is more segregated along Protestant-Catholic lines than at any point before the Good Friday Agreement (Garrigan, 2011). For Christians enmeshed in sectarianism, the irony is that in each community using religion to stake territory as 'my home and not your home', home *in God* is ignored. As noted in the Introduction, nationalism is a common salve to the pain of the 'gap of the now': dressing it up as religiosity does not make it any more fulfilling. On the contrary, seeing nationalism as a salve makes any feeling of belonging in God's creation less accessible because the violence and hatred generated by sectarianism become yet further evidence of God's non-presence in 'this world'; and disdain for 'enemies' is allegedly justified.

In its context of Roman imperial rule over settled communities, the New Testament specifically calls those seen as other 'enemies'. For example, Matt 5:43–44: 'You have heard that it was said, "You shall love your neighbour and hate your enemy." But I say to you, Love your enemies and pray for those who persecute you.' Enemies are not usually temporary – indeed, they are usually long-lasting – and so with this emphasis, Jesus's teaching closes the potential loophole of loving only those who need short harbour in one's midst; those like the temporarily displaced foreigner. Indeed, all sorts of seemingly permanent distinctions between humans are to be eradicated by this love of enemies. 'In that renewal there is no longer Greek and Jew, circumcised and uncircumcised, barbarian, Scythian, slave and free; but Christ is all and in all!' (Col 3:11). The very notion of otherness is undercut.

As José Ramirez Kidd argues, whatever word is used or however it is used, 'otherness' is also the key to understanding the Hebrew Bible's divine commands regarding non-Israelites, and prejudice and discrimination against the other are what it outlaws (1999). Jesus maintains this. Asked by a lawyer which commandment is the greatest, Jesus replies by quoting the law, the Torah – '"You shall love the Lord your God with all your heart, and with all your soul, and with all your mind." This is the greatest and first commandment. And a second is like it: "You shall love your neighbour as yourself"' (Matthew 22:37–39, quoting Deuteronomy 6:5 and Leviticus 19:18). 'Love' – *agape* – in the ancient near east inferred a skill (or a set of skills), not, as in the modern West, a sentiment. Therefore, to answer the question of *how* to love one's enemies, we can suggest it is, following Gafney, by forming and sustaining actual relationships with the people you think of as opposed to you, a threat to you, or just unpleasantly different to you. It is about making neighbours out of enemies, it is about transforming one's sense of one another 'one relationship at a time'. Doing so alters one's idea of home.

3.4 Problematic Neighbours

For the Hebrew Bible's audiences, 'neighbour' meant something specific, a particular form of social relationship. So when Leviticus commands: 'Love your neighbour as yourself' (19:18), the text has to spell out how to cut a field in such a way as to act 'lovingly', but it does not have to spell out what the concept of neighbour means; it means 'members of your community'. However, in today's Global North, the word 'neighbour' does not necessarily mean this. It is increasingly common not even to know the names of one's neighbours, never mind anything about them, and instead to find community through networks of association unrelated to physical location or kinship. The temptation is to define community membership quite narrowly, and this is seen nowhere more than in churches. Where once Christians gathered according to denomination, they increasingly choose specific congregations that express their politics, often along lines that track culture wars.

One theological challenge created by this 'echo-chamber' approach to community is that most modern Westerners shy away from calling 'enemies' by that name. As Alistair McFadyen has argued, many Christians even see not having enemies as virtuous; but in avoiding admitting that we have enemies, we avoid the responsibility to love them. Once we admit enmity and name enemies, we can develop the necessary skills to love them. McFadyen suggests a better approach for Christians: '"solidarity", "love" and "justice" might be read together as indicating an alternative way of having enemies without attendant demonization or dehumanisation, rather than as an alternative to having enemies' (2013: 17). Moreover, McFadyen offers striking examples of the skills involved in this view of 'love' from his work in urban policing, such as how it can translate into practices of treating prisoners with dignity or of operating minimal physical restraint when detaining them.

Another specific skill is suggested by the poet Gail McConnell, whose Protestant father was killed by the IRA in front of her Belfast home when she was three years old. Speaking of her mother's Christian faith, she reflects that 'grace and forgiveness were her way through this ... And one of the things I think that those theological ideas can do is to encourage you to imagine the lives of other people, including the lives of those who some might call your enemies ... from an early age, I was encouraged to think and imagine about this event from – as it were – "the other side", or from the perspective of those who had chosen to do it' (McConnell, 2021). Imagining the lives of others, including those who would kill you, is a powerful witness to a very specific Way in the midst of sectarian societies, where enmity can be so intractable that it is 'normal', and so many children – unlike McConnell – are raised to regard certain neighbours as normatively 'enemies'. But 'imagining the lives of others' with kindness, research, and understanding is also a way to love neighbours in contexts other than sectarian or estranged ones – and there are many of them – where it is simply not safe to invite 'just anyone' in for a cup of tea and a chat.

The specificity of the term 'neighbour' in denoting the challenge of forging an actual relationship across the boundaries of difference is taken up perhaps most famously by Sjören Kierkegaard. Exploring the dialectic between 'neighbourly' love (for strangers/enemies) and 'preferential' love (for family/friends),

Kierkegaard insists that neighbourly love is the greater, because it informs preferential love and not, as was the opinion of his contemporaries, the other way around. This is because preferential love is susceptible to endemic selfishness; as Matt Rosen puts it, 'the Other of a preferential love relation is "*for*-me": the manifestation of their qualities is *from* me', whereas 'The Other who is loved as a stranger is an Other who is loved without regard to their identities, positions in society, etc.' (2019: 2). What makes such neighbourly love possible, in Kierkegaard's schema, is divine love: 'in love for the neighbor, God is the middle term' (Rosen, 2019: 1) – although precisely how God might be this middle term is open to diverse interpretation. One compelling interpretation comes from Janna Gonwa, who turns to Augustine's maxim in *De Trinitate* that God 'loves us in order that we might become', to suggest that such an understanding 'grounds love for the neighbour in her particular individuality as she is being called into fellowship with God, rather than in the application of a universal ethical law or as a by-product of the believer's obligation to Christ' (2015: 84).

Such a conclusion has a lot in common with Gafney's analysis of Deuteronomy 7:12–11:25. Loving the stranger is accomplished not by fulfilling minimal civic obligations towards them but by relationship, by mutual encounter over time. But it also extends Gafney's observation by making clear that it is divine-human participation that makes such relating possible. This is a critical point for this Element, because while it is divine love that supplies the necessary transformative power to love, it is only through loving others that we 'become'. As 1 John 4:19–21 has it,

> We love because he first loved us. Those who say, 'I love God', and hate their brothers or sisters, are liars; for those who do not love a brother or sister whom they have seen, cannot love God whom they have not seen. The commandment we have from him is this: those who love God must love their brothers and sisters also.

Participating in the life of God is thus revealed to have a dual aspect: we are pulled into participation by divine love and pushed into participation by actually loving our neighbours, simultaneously.

And so in addition to celebrating life and caring for strangers, actually loving one's neighbours – one relationship at a time, not denying enmity, imagining the lives of others – is the key practical and dispositional *dynamic* for participating in the life of God, and so for being at home, now. But loving one's neighbours can be terribly difficult and, as I have argued elsewhere, what can make doing so possible is prayer (Garrigan, 2022). Loving one's neighbour *is* participation in the life of God. The alternative – hating or avoiding enemies – results in feelings of endless fear and isolation, stoking the imagination of human-divine belonging as 'elsewhere' and not enjoying the process of participating in it now. I have come to find one additional bible story – the Road to Emmaus – insightful in this regard because of its naming the stranger to be loved as a 'companion'.

3.5 Companionship

One of the things I loved about leading Coventry's Emmaus community for people experiencing homelessness (I was its founding Director, from 1993 to 1996), was that everyone who lived there was called a 'companion', whatever their station in life. We were only the second Emmaus community to be established in the UK and so we followed quite closely the practices of the many well-established communities in France. Although Parisians had called the original community members *chiffoniers* – rag-pickers – because of the recycling work that is still the engine of the Emmaus way of life, the organisation's now-discredited founder, L'abbé Pierre, called everyone his *compagnon/e*, and the name became, and remains, the formal term for community members. I found 'companion' a very useful term. It reminded me that for all that leadership and management was my particular role, my main purpose there was to accompany – and to be accompanied. Even though using the word took British and Irish people a little getting used to, many people who were used to being known primarily as 'homeless' or 'client' or 'service-user' enjoyed the reorientation offered by the term. It said they were wanted for their companionship, rather than being defined by their problems.

Evidently, the story of Christ's post-resurrection appearance to his followers on the road to Emmaus was the inspiration for our organisation's name (Luke 23:13–35). One explanation for this is that the disciples offer the Christ figure not just food and shelter, but also conversation, interest, and companionship in walking. But perhaps a stronger reason is that the two disciples walking the road invite their companion to stay with them *as a stranger*, with no notion that he is the risen Christ: 'As they came near the village to which they were going, he walked ahead as if he were going on. But they urged him strongly, saying, "Stay with us, because it is almost evening and the day is now nearly over." So he went in to stay with them' (Luke 24:28–31). Only as the stranger went on to bless and break bread did the disciples realise they had in fact looked after Christ on their way to Emmaus. Due to divisive experiences with proselytising in post-war Paris, the original Emmaus Community determined after its first year (1949) that the organisation would keep its name but have no religious affiliation, and proselytising would be one of only two proscribed activities (the other: bringing drugs/alcohol onsite). In this proscription, the Emmaus Community confirmed its distinctive reading of Luke's story: we are companions to others *as they are* and we must not seek to change them to make them acceptable to us.

Coventry's Emmaus Community, like those in France, was thus predicated on radical acceptance: people joined on a first-come, first-served basis. There was no vetting, no waiting list, and no time-limit on a stay. If a room was available, it was yours for as long as you wanted it; many companions stay for a long time and some even for life. It offered an open-ended offer of a home. Having encountered other agencies charged with tackling homelessness before coming to Emmaus, this ethic appealed to me enormously. The churches and shelters where I had worked previously were staffed by kind people but were hidebound by target demographics and target move-on dates. Moreover, in addition to the accent on companionship at Emmaus, another on work (everyone worked, according to their abilities, either in the house/gardens or the recycling/restoration business, supported by a team of volunteer experts) ensured that people gained satisfaction not just from having the sense of purpose that meaningful work can bring but also from knowing that we were earning the means by which the house and daily life were paid for.

However, radical acceptance was very difficult to accept. The local neighbourhood in Coventry objected strongly to our lack of vetting, arguing that by potentially accommodating people on the sex-offenders register we were putting local children at risk. The local council objected on the grounds of safeguarding when a mother-father couple moved in with their two (and third on-the-way) children. A former sex-worker found the male-dominated environment unconducive to her recovery and advocated for a female-only wing – which was impossible to supply with a gender-blind admissions policy and so few bedrooms (twelve at first, later sixteen). And myself, I found the challenge of accepting whoever showed up very difficult – and revealing about my biases. Irish and Scottish people, alcoholics, people of colour, elderly people, frustrated creatives, people suffering from depression, road-men from the Abbey circuits, women, LGBTQ people, and any (rare) person with a driving licence: easy! Drug dealers, people experiencing schizophrenia, people with convictions for serious violence, young people straight out of care, fundamentalist Christians, former British military: this is where using the word 'companion' reminded me of my task.

To accompany, and be accompanied, is a different mode of relating than the potentially condescending 'helping' of typical Christian charity, but it is also productively different to 'encountering', which can be a little distant, and 'befriending', which cannot be done to order. I cherish the friendships I made at Emmaus but, like any friendships, they took time to develop and were only possible with a fraction of the people I met. However, everyone I met there 'loved' me, and taught me something, *through their companionship*. Did the disciples on the road to Emmaus help Jesus, or befriend him? Neither, really, but they were companions to him, as he was to them. Furthermore, to term 'loving your neighbour' as accompanying and being accompanied is also helpfully different to 'solidarity', primarily because it is less abstract, but also because solidarity too often also ends up meaning 'helping' or sharing normative views/values. Mutual companionship is a way of describing a mode of relating that insists on maintaining the equal dignity of all parties, challenging the power dynamics and so inhabiting a divine instead of a top-down paradigm of how the world is ordered.

3.6 As Yourself

As the people on the road to Emmaus walked and talked and blessed and broke bread that night, so the practice of accompanying one another can draw humans, now, as participants into the life of God, for mutual companionship is God's work in the world. This was revealed by the eating habits of the post-resurrection Christ, just as it had been fundamental to the laws given in the Hebrew Bible. Mutual companionship thus constitutes participation in the divine life when we reach, often clumsily and always vulnerably, for ways to accompany and be accompanied across the boundaries of difference/otherness; and for those times there are the skills mentioned earlier to aid and reassure us.

In some Christian traditions, there are also skills, as well as inspiration and guidance, available in the companionship offered by the Communion of Saints. The dominant version of 'saints' through modernity has followed a 'patronage' model, whereby Christians on earth appeal to saints in heaven to intercede for them, with God, to gain what they pray for. It is a devotional practice with foundations not in the Bible but in the client-patron system of the late Roman Empire. However, there is an alternative, 'companionship model' of saints offered in the Bible, rooted in 'the cloud of witnesses' (Hebrews 12:1), Paul's many references to disciples as saints (living and dead), biblical prophets through the ages, and the early church's view of Mary. According to Elizabeth Johnson, 'In the companionship model ... the chief practice is attending to the memory of the dead in a way that energizes hope ... such remembering disrupts the tyranny of the present status quo, summons up a future worth struggling for and sets our feet on the path of their unfinished business' (Johnson, 2000). Not only does this view of the saints as companions potentially 'help' Christians to practise companionship – through the memory of their struggles and love of God – it also alerts them (as with discipleship) to the essentially eschatological nature of the enterprise. The intersubjectivity of divine life is what gives it this eschatological character, rooting those living in the now as home (and not gap) in the memories and hopes of those who have lived before them and those who are yet to come. The communion of saints in this understanding assures Christians that the task of companionship is not a wheel we have to invent; it is a history, a present, and a future that we are called – commanded – to inhabit with those we find ourselves with.

The 'greatest command' is not, 'Get your house in order for the afterlife.' It is, 'Love God, and love your neighbour as yourself.' They are linked, God and neighbour and self, such that by loving those we might prefer not to love, enabled by divine love, we participate in the life of God, here and now. One's house might not thus ever be in order, but one's home is assured.

4 Sacramentality

To live sacramentally is to participate in the life of God and thus to be at home. Sacramentality is here understood as the theological idea that the body of Christ is present in the world not merely in terms of a metaphysical claim to divine incarnation in the historical Jesus, but as a cosmic, multifaceted, current, and ongoing aspect of all bodily life, animated by the Holy Spirit. To speak of sacramentality is then to affirm, as Mary Veeneman does, that 'At their core, sacraments are physical things that, in some way, make spiritual realities present' (2017: 363). To live sacramentally is to encounter those realities, in the world and in one another, and by doing so, to feel an adequate sense of belonging in the here and now.

Admittedly, the theological articulation of sacramentality has a damaged reputation, having been overly focused on discussion of 'the sacraments' as a limited number of specific rituals and thereby misconstrued at times to instrumentalise God's grace, endow clerics with undue power, undergird misogyny, exert social exclusion, and generally substantiate the mistake identified in Section 1 as 'belonging as accumulation of capital' (**i**). Would it not therefore be better to find an alternative – and more historically ecumenical – term for this third outworking of the theology of home that I want to suggest? Perhaps, but I have not been able to find a different term that so clearly makes the link between God's work in creation and salvation history and God's present availability as home for creatures in every moment of their earthly lives. Sacramentality is the word in Christian tradition for a felt sense or embodied knowledge of divine belonging that has the power to assure humans of their *current* home in God. Moreover, the term is utilised across an increasing array of Christianity's various traditions and so has nascent ecumenical appeal. Therefore, with others, I hope to rehabilitate this term.

To that end, this section draws on the critical treatments of sacramentality in recent constructive theologies, Louis-Marie Chauvet's in particular, and corrals from these theologies potential elements for a theology of home.

4.1 Reimagining Sacramentality

The late twentieth and early twenty-first centuries have brought radical developments in sacramental theologies. Some Protestant traditions that previously de-emphasised or even denied sacramentality have reassessed its history and reclaimed for it a wider relevance (e.g., Boersma, 2011; Brewer, 2017), Orthodox traditions have re-articulated it for ecumenical and ecological purposes (e.g., Zizioulas, 1985; Chryssavgis, 2019), and Catholic traditions – where the academic discussion was for a long time primarily located – have undergone radical developments in how they understand it, some of which will be considered next.

What has opened up these possibilities is a move from a univocal to an analogous view of sacramentality. Accordingly, where once there were thought to be a set number of strictly scripted rites that were exclusively classed as sacraments (e.g., two for Lutherans, seven for Roman Catholics), and these were seen as discrete mechanisms for delivering special access to divine grace (as a sort of fuel from the home from which we came and to which we longed to return), there emerged through the twentieth century a broadening in how sacramentality was understood – an 'analogous' framing – such that things that were not strictly numerable rites of the church were affirmed as being sacrament-like. Thus, Karl Rahner (1963) described the church itself as a sacrament, and Vatican II affirmed Christ as 'the primordial sacrament' (*Sacrosanctum concilium*, 1962: 14) – a position not wholly unlike Karl Barth's late-life conclusion that *only* Christ is a sacrament (Currie, 2016). The Catholic view of sacraments was simultaneously substantially developed by Edward Schillebeeckx's redefinition of them as 'encounters', personalising the concept and forefronting the particularity and embodied nature of the individual's lived experience (1963).

Post-Vatican II, an analogous, rather than univocal, definition of sacraments has most recently focused on the Word as sacrament, and this is of special relevance to a theology of home. The Word that was made flesh and dwelt among us, the Word that is God's revelation in Christ and in scripture, has not always been a route for thinking about what sacramentality is or what it might mean to live sacramentally, that is, with/in the Word. Consequently, how biblical texts can be encountered as sacramental is currently being explored to explicitly ecumenical ends (Baldovin, 2018). This is a far cry from the popular orthodoxies of sacramental theology in early modernity wherein Protestants could accuse Catholics of believing in magic and Catholics could accuse Protestants of denying divine presence. It is also a far cry from Tridentine arguments about transubstantiation and all the horrors that ensued. But, as Rhodora Beaton remarks, these recent developments represent something even more radical: in addition to their ecumenical value, they offer 'a deeper understanding of sacramentality – the recognition of God's grace present in the world in diverse ways' (2014: 2). Thus, sacramentality has come to be understood as the contextual and particular work of the Spirit, and grace comes into focus as immanent: home in the now.

However, there is a tension in the aforementioned theological developments, as in this Element, between recognising that humans encounter God's grace through a diverse range of experiences or encounters and maintaining the longstanding root of sacramental theology in specific rites of the Church, Baptism and Eucharist especially. Is God encountered/does God reveal Godself sacramentally *only* via worship? There is a risk for theologians who do not start with the authorised rituals of institutional churches that they will be criticised for not rooting their methodology in liturgical praxis or, worse, that their theology is in some way heterodox. Thus, Graham Hughes's posthumously published *Reformed Sacramentality* affirms that 'Faith depends on materiality', but insists that Christians learn this *through* the sacraments of the church (2017: 168). This tension is not entirely new. Since the 1980s, some theologians have posited as their starting point an affirmation of sacramentality as a wide and deep phenomenon, greater than the rites which traditionally were held to access it. Bernard Cooke, for example, argued that there is a 'basic sacramentality of Christian life that grounds the meaning and effectiveness of the liturgical rituals. Understanding, appreciating, and living out this sacramentality is, I believe, the most important element in the development of Christian spirituality' (1983: vi). None of the aforementioned authors denies that it is via a community of faith that Christians are formed, and sustained, but is it *only* via the rituals of institutional churches that sacramentality is accessed? Is it only by participating in the formal sacraments of the church that one can inhabit the home that sacramentality offers in the world?

4.2 The Linguistic Turn

Louis-Marie Chauvet navigated this tension by setting out to supply, 'a foundational theology of sacramentality' (1995: 1), while affirming the 'distinct sacraments' of the church as '*symbolic figures allowing us entrance into, and empowerment to live out, the (arch-)sacramentality which is the very essence of*

Christian existence' (1995: 2). In combat with what he sees as a discredited onto-theological model of cause and effect, Chauvet uses the 'turn to language' to re-articulate the sacraments in terms of symbolic mediation: if human existence is mediated entirely through language, then within language must lie the nexus of divine-human mediation. Accordingly, there is no 'direct access' for a human to the divine (or to anything); all encounters and all meaning is dependent on language. And so, rather than looking to the mediatory power of a priest or metaphysical 'mysteries' or the church to understand sacramentality, Chauvet looks to the ways that language, especially through ritual, mediates God's presence and work in the world.

However, it is not primarily verbal language or its uses that Chauvet has in mind. He understands the body, embodiment itself, *all* bodies, as language: 'corporality is the body's very speech' and, as such, corporality is the discernible locus of the work of the Spirit in the world (1995: 146). Bodies for Chauvet involve physical human bodies but are understood to be constituted by 'the symbolic order' which also includes cultures, histories, traditions and, of course, verbal languages. The Word of God is, then, always 'at the mercy of the body' (Chauvet, 2001). Within this embodied vision of sacramentality, the sacraments of the church are '*one element among others* in this vast and yet coherent psychic structure which all together makes up Christian identity ... a series of connections between Scripture (the level of cognition), sacrament (the level of thanksgiving), and ethics (the level of action)' (1995: 3). With this schema, Chauvet shifts theology's focus from *the* sacraments to the sacramen*tal*, opening up a sacramental interpretation of the entirety of the created order, and of what it means to lead a Christian life within such a frame.

At root, Chauvet wants to reinstate a view of God's entire creation as sacramental in the face of a history of sacramental theology that repeatedly tended to instrumentalise divine grace. Chauvet's main objection is to the long-standing Roman Catholic view of sacraments as grace-dispensers in a transactional imagination of salvation: if priests do x in a specific way, God will do y to the compliant Christians who assent to the priests. But he also sees something instrumentalising at play in more recent and apparently critical versions, such as Barth's, because if sacraments are mere signs of a gift already bestowed on humans, then they are transmitters of a message to a nonetheless passive recipient rather than creative/generative moments of what Schillebeeckx insisted were in fact divine 'encounters' – events that invited, even demanded, *participation* by humans. Chauvet's understanding that the Word of God is at the mercy of the body therefore shifts a focus not only from the sacraments to the sacramental but also within Western conceptualisation of the divine, because it amounts to a particular claim about the sort of God who would assent to work through the corporality of the created order, humans included. Fundamentally, understanding the Word of God to be at the mercy of the body opens up a view of creaturely life as participation in divine life, now, in the created order rather than the previous prevalent idea of God at-a-distance. In doing so, it offers a further route for reimagining what it means to be at home with God in the world.

4.3 Sacramental Diversity

It is this view of creaturely life as participation in the life of God, bringing with it an emphasis not only on encounter but also on immanent transcendence (Rahner, 1978), the contextual contingency of symbols/rituals (Chauvet, 1995; Boeve, 2018), and the sheer creativity opened up by language as the medium of God's self-giving (Power, 1998), that allows for recognition of sacramental diversity remarked earlier. Examples of such diversity can be found in recent studies that – to name but a few – view the Universe as God's body and all within it as potentially sacramental (McFague, 1993), call for an East-West 'everyday' interpretation of what it is 'to be eucharistic' (McLoughlin, 2022), and see 'Creation as Sacrament' (Chryssavgis, 2019) – although Chryssavgis is keen to point out that since the Orthodox Church never numbered its sacraments, he is accenting a sacramental diversity his church always already understood.

But of particular relevance to this Element is the diversity in burgeoning uses of 'sacramentality' in a range of contexts that would not previously have adopted the term – for example, womanist claims of hospitality as sacramental (Westfield, 2001), a number of Non-Conformist works on preaching as sacramental (e.g., Jong, 2020), and feminist claims of classroom teaching as sacramental (Buchannan, 2011). The diversity of traditions using the term helps to overcome a longstanding division (between 'sacramental' and 'non-sacramental' denominations), which matters to the idea of home because so much of the logic of Christian othering has been learned vis-a-vis other Christians. But more than that, the expansions to the term involved in these various uses of it tell us something about 'home'.

For example, several studies of contemporary music worship suggest it is sacramental because the experience for worshippers is a communally mediated encounter with God's presence, a glimpse of and an encouragement to their participation in the life of God. These studies consider worship experiences that do not involve conventionally defined 'sacraments', such as evangelical Praise and Worship services (Koenig, 2008), Pentecostal services (Portugal, 2020), and online choirs recording contemporary Christian music during Covid (Johnson and Thiessen, 2023), and they propose a potential usefulness for the term 'sacramental' in describing the theological significance of these services. Emily Snider Andrews draws on ethno-musicology as well as the post-modern sacramental theologies outlined earlier to suggest that Christian worship conducted through contemporary worship music should be considered sacramental. She argues that by 'prioritizing sensory forms, the body, and both collective and individual experiences of meaning as fundamental sites for encountering the divine ... the God-encounter is understood and legitimated through phenomenological examinations of religious practice, practices that have become increasingly mediated and mediatized for many evangelical worshipers through modern worship music' (2017: 102). Andrews's argument cuts two ways: it proposes that what she terms as 'elites' in traditionally sacramental churches have no exclusive rights to self-identify by use of the term nor are they justified in portraying evangelical worship as somehow 'lesser' in terms of its access to divine grace. At the same time, considering the merits of framing modern Christian music as 'sacramental' suggests to evangelical and other churches that have spurned the term that they are missing out on the significant theological value of adopting it. She proposes that: 'By valuing the embodied, event-nature of worship and the worshiper's lived experience, one is empowered to take seriously the evangelical's claims about encountering God in the music of worship' (2017: 105). Naming these experiences as 'sacramental' affirms a greater range of ways of participating in the life of God than had previously been understood and, because it creates a unity across a diversity of expressions that were once thought 'sacramental/non-sacramental', it expands the Christian imagination of 'home'.

But are there limits to an analogical use of the term 'sacramental'? Could it not be claimed that *all* music is potentially sacramental? What about poetry or art? Music being such a huge part of my own life, through both Irish traditional music and Anglican choral music at Evensong (another service long described as 'non-sacramental'), I should be favourably disposed to accepting such a proposal. Making the case for 'art as sacrament', Marcel Bernard determines that for it to be so, it must be brought into 'a Christian discourse as it is transferred in tradition, liturgy and Holy Scripture. After all, this discourse speaks about the concrete and institutional Church as "the body of Christ"' (2019: 28). But there are two problems inherent in such a prescription. The first is that quite a lot of Christians meet barriers in the institutional Church precisely at the point it celebrates the body of Christ.

Serious barriers to participation in the church's sacraments exist for – to name but a few – LGBTQ people (Garrigan, 2009), people who have been barred from receiving the sacraments (e.g., divorcees in the RC Church), and people who cannot get to church. There are also many people who have been abused in church contexts (plus their families and friends) and people repelled from Christianity by the sectarianism in which they were raised. These latter, while not excluded from sacramental participation by church authorities, are alienated from it because of their experiences. Moreover, perhaps the barrier to participation in liturgy that affects the largest number of people in the West is felt by people who cannot tolerate the misogyny manifest in the persistently masculine language for God and, in many churches, the ban on women in sacramental ministries. As Susan Ross exposes, a feminist approach to sacramental theology must heed the ambiguities produced by this barrier, ranging from the grief of those who want to participate but cannot in good faith do so to the creativity of those who yet find ways to do so within or outside the official liturgies – or both (Ross, 1998).

The second problem in Bernard's theory is that, even though it is based in Chauvet's schema of scripture-sacrament-ethics, it forgets ethics. Bernard was inspired by how a site-specific artwork in a specific church evoked the memory of thousands of people buried there and tells how a litany during an Advent Eucharist referenced the dead of the artwork and evoked in an abstract way 'the horrors' of the world. In doing so, he claims art as sacramental because of its rich aesthetic power to render 'presence from absence' and not by linking it to the actual ethical demands on the congregation. The same problem is apparent when claims about contemporary worship music as sacramental do not include a reckoning with the mainstream Christian music industry (part of a Christian retail industry estimated to be worth $5billion annually in the United States alone) and its capitalist ethics (McGinnis, 2023), or the part it plays in specific, globalised right-wing political programmes. Moreover, a focus on the experience of divine encounter without articulation of the ethical framework to which it binds a person risks returning sacramental theology to 'interiority' as the locus of divine action, God being 'received' by the believer in a moment of grace instead of the believer being drawn ever closer in ongoing participation in God's life in the world.

Taking the two tensions together, the question becomes then: if sacramentality is a term for a diverse set of ways of describing 'how God's presence is made sense-able in our world' (Andrews, 2017: 96), what are the criteria for deciding what is sacramental and what is not? To examine this question fully lies beyond the scope of this Element, but for the purposes of the following argument, I adopt Leonardo Boff's approach. He sees 'the world as a sacrament of God' (1998: 8) and affirms that anything can be a sacrament, wherein 'the transcendent breaks through into the immanent' (1998: 24) to provide human encounter with God's loving grace. But he points out that in order to perceive something as a sacrament one must be looking with 'the eyes of faith', that is: eyes that have been formed to see the ethics demanded by such encounters, the communities to which it connects and obligates us; the human politics that demand divine kenosis. In such a view, sacramentality – like the arrival of strangers – is more often than not challenging to and destabilising of our view of ourselves or the world.

4.4 The Sacramentality of Home

Living sacramentally involves seeking to recognise God's ongoing presence even and perhaps especially in the absences presented by exclusion, erasure, ecological collapse, and all else of life that is, to echo the Prodigal's father, 'lost and not yet found'. For this to work, sacramentality cannot be thought of as the sole preserve of ecclesial authorities – even as it may be learned there. Rather, sacramentality is God's ongoing revelation via matter, the body, all that is created. As Lieven Boeve points out, 'This is the paradox of Christian revelation: the God who never can be contained by the historical and material, nevertheless only reveals Godself in the concrete here and now' (2018: 157). Such a reinterpretation of sacramentality might reimagine 'home' in at least four ways.

First, it offers a strong corrective to 'the gap of the now' identified in Section 1. It is a salve to the anxiety of exile produced by that 'gap' because it assures humans that God did not somehow abandon them in this time of earthly existence and instead remains intimately connected to them. As Chauvet puts it, a sacramental view of existence reveals God to be living 'among us', not 'above us' (1995: 534). Furthermore, sacramentality affirms humans' earthly existence as being fully at home with God because it reveals God precisely in and through the very earthiness of their existence. Sacramentality thus repositions humans as participants in the divine life precisely because they are part of the created order and thus God's ongoing work of creation. Human belonging can then be reimagined simply by living as an animal, not having to assume a non-human state (pre-birth, post-death) to be at home with God. Sacramentality causes the pain of separation induced by the gap of the now to be replaced with a deep sense of belonging.

Second, it refuses the idea, popular in self-help culture, that one's individual human body is one's 'home', without rejecting the significance of the body. It is through one's body that a human being lives in the world, but Christians are part of a sacramental body that can only be understood, like Christ's, as threefold. As Chauvet puts it, 'This is what is implied by the concept of *corporality:* one's own physical body certainly, but *as the place where* the triple body – social, ancestral, and cosmic – which makes up the subject is symbolically joined, in an original manner for each one of us according to the different forms of our desires' (1995: 150). At another point, Chauvet maps this 'threefold' as 'culture, tradition, and nature' (1995: 150). Either way, sacramentality is construed as a way of recognising the intersubjectivity of human life, and individualistic conceptions of human living are resisted. Living sacramentally furnishes a sense of belonging, now, to a massive web of connections and of learning to trust that in fact there can be no 'gap'; our lives are inseparable from those who have gone before us and those alive at the same time as us. Yes, we can choose to separate from parts that are harmful to us (family, church, etc.), but we will yet retain massive connectivity.

Third, it acknowledges ritual/worship/liturgy, broadly understood, as a distinct route to understanding oneself to be already living at home with God. At an earlier stage in my life, I argued that it can be productive to think of liturgy *as* home (Garrigan, 2017), but I have come to see that claim as too idealistic because, as noted earlier, many Christians are excluded from or repelled by their ecclesial communities; churches can do great harm. However, I still view liturgy as a privileged topos for political theology because it, uniquely, directs people to the body via the Logos in their midst in a public milieu – and makes it available for analysis, criticism, and accountability. So, where liturgical participation is possible, it can *show a way* home – we can *feel at home* in worship/liturgy and, in doing so, recognise what it is to be at home in the cosmos. As such, the nation – or the TV fantasies – lose their appeal and their power. And as Susan Ross brought to light, and as I myself experienced in the New York Women's Liturgy Group, liturgies are not necessarily confined to institutional settings. For those whose circumstances allow, liturgies can be wrought over time with a group of companions and form more than adequate contexts of belonging.

Fourth, it sees the sacramental as the *oikos* – house/home – that reconnects us within the *oikumene* – the whole of the inhabited earth, and thus challenges the ways that interfaith and intrafaith divisions can mimic nationalistic ones. Ecumenism becomes the context of sacramentality. As such it models an alternative belonging to the very powerful force that is nationalism, especially when it is laminated with Christianity. Christian nationalism requires a racialised religiosity to thrive – as seen with sectarianism in Ireland, or the fantasy of Protestant-only governance in current revivals of US Christian nationalism; ditto *Ruski Mir* as part of a distinctively *Russian* branch of the Orthodox Church. Sacramentality then must be very carefully understood; sacramental participation may occur within a specific faith-group but the home it indicates is with the entirety of the created order, by the power of a Spirit that knows no bounds. The denomination in which worship occurs must not be mistaken, as it so often has been, for divine belonging or national legitimation.

Conclusion

To prevent homelessness, home must ultimately be understood in terms of participating in the life of God. In such a theology, home becomes a verb rather than a noun. The verb it becomes is awkward to express in the English language: 'homing' is usually used only for pigeons, and there it implies a top-down hierarchy of 'taming' that is antithetical to the arguments propounded here. The activity indicated as 'home' in this Element is instead rendered as 'participating' and much of what it involves is 'rejecting possession'. The dispositions of discipleship, companionship, and sacramental attunement outlined in the preceding three sections *discipline* humans simultaneously to reject possession and to participate in divine life. Living in these ways shapes not only our imaginations but also, in time, our concrete realities. What then are the implications of this idea of home in concrete terms? How does it move a government to build more social and cost-rental housing? How does it counter racist attitudes towards migrants? What does it mean for a Christian's personal housing choices and uses?

Can a Theology of Home End Homelessness?

The ideas in this Element, obviously, are not intended as public policy for combatting homelessness. To accomplish that, the social sciences have already suggested the 'housing first' approach and economics has suggested the unitary housing model. According to these policy proposals, if the social and cost-rental housing sector constituted at least 25 per cent of the housing market, it would compete with the private sector and regulate it (Goldrick-Kelly and Taft, 2023). And if people experiencing homelessness were given *housing first* (i.e., before other personal needs are addressed), the duration of their homelessness would lessen and their ability to get back on their feet would improve (O'Sullivan, 2020). Yet in most Anglophone countries, the unitary housing model is a theory, not a practice, and a 'housing first' approach has been adopted patchily in some places and not at all in others – in part because the requisite social housing and cost-rental housing stock is not available. For a long time, we have known what policies would end homelessness, but our governments have not implemented them. Indeed, our representatives have persistently chosen other approaches, ones based on possession, ownership, private gain – and charity for those people whom these approaches inevitably exclude.

One reason the economic unitary model has not been implemented is that it goes against a normative set of assumptions about 'home' which have deep and theologically inflected roots. Those roots lie in the insecurity inflicted by 'the gap of the now' and the resultant habit of relying on the six false 'belongings' outlined in Section 1: consumer capitalism, respectability-signalling, entitlement for the superior, possession (and racialised ordering of human life), patriarchy, and nationalism. In particular, the assumptions about 'home' that developed through colonial modernity as 'a new form of possessive logic' still today form the basis of Western social norms (Jennings, 2019: 398). Likewise, a 'housing first' approach goes against the long-standing assumption that people experiencing homelessness must have quite a lot wrong with them, an assumption that simultaneously denies the political and economic causes of homelessness and allows the majority to pretend that this suffering could not happen to them. Such a common consensus about the needs of 'the homeless' is based on perceiving people experiencing homelessness as inferior and it has led to all manner of programmes designed to fix people's health or skill-set or addictions, and so on, *as a route to* tackling homelessness.

Theology's role then is to 'correct the record' such that the public mindset is oriented towards, instead of against, implementing these policies. Theology can inform and, I hope, alter public expectations when it comes to home by giving people the means and the courage to alter their idea of home, to change how they respond to homelessness, and to shape future policy. Society needs to imagine *collective* forms of life if a unitary housing model is to be implemented; and to do this, Western societies will need to let go of their attachment to possession as a right. Theology can help to accomplish this, because theology helped to shape the false belongings, the mistaken ideas of home, in the first place. But theology can also help accomplish this because it has viable alternative ideas which have been proven effective in supporting a common life where they have been given a chance, as will be discussed next.

Similarly, theology's ability to counter racist responses to migrants, or to the racialised other at the root of religious sectarianism, can form and reform people's ideas through its critiques of whiteness, extractivism, and of religion itself. Theology can argue persuasively for certain ecological ideas that impel people to take action both to limit the impending catastrophe and to care for those affected by it (e.g., Gebara, 1999; Francis, 2015). Theology can call out false Christianity in its nationalist and capitalist forms (e.g., Rieger, 2018). Theology can resist racism and offer alternative visions (e.g., Jennings, 2010). Theology can bear witness to the need to treat migrants well, not only by saying that 'aggression is a mistake' but also by naming the many ways that Christianity's own history has discovered that rejecting the other is self-defeating in the long run, as well as by telling the histories of Christianity's many non-violent, hate-resisting, and community-building interventions. It can alter anti-immigrant sentiment by listening to local communities' legitimate concerns and, by working at grassroots level and through education, honour the distinction between implementation of migration policy and racism against migrants (Hargaden, 2023). And theology must do all the aforementioned via all available forms, not least: preaching, op-ed writing, broadcasting, social media interventions, and, perhaps especially, through its rituals (Garrigan, 2010).

But to do all of this, theology needs to have un-thought home as something previous and subsequent to 'the gap of the now' (which inevitably leads to the pain of separation and the protection of seemingly scarce resources), and it needs to have re-thought it in line with the biblical record. It needs to be able to articulate that home is not something one possesses (like property in capitalism) or aligns to (like the state in nationalism), but something in which one participates. Theology can, perhaps uniquely, influence social attitudes by bearing witness to what it has known from its Jewish roots right through to (locally to me) its British-Irish sectarian 'Troubles': participation in the divine life is not possible if you hate your neighbours or fear strangers or refuse to find mutual companionship with those who are different to you. Such attitudes separate us not only from one another but also from our current, available home in God, creating endless cycles of homelessness.

Home as a Verb

We have established what sort of home a Christian might have theologically: participation in the life of God. But of what, then, ought a home to consist for a Christian in material terms? Like everything else with Christianity, it will depend on context but, whatever the context, it will reject possession. So fundamental a structuring thought-form of our times is possession that it will require great imagination to think and act differently, but such an imagination can be cultivated through the practices of discipleship, companionship, and sacramentality. It is not that these three things tell us the sort of house one ought to live in; it is that these three things become home and then other things – including housing choices, where choice exists – follow from living in these ways. The power of these disciplines in cultivating particular sensibilities and shaping particular dispositions becomes much more apparent when they are expressed as verbs: *following* Jesus/*being* a disciple, mutually *accompanying*, and *meeting* God by *living* sacramentally. They do so even more when we articulate the verbs they counter: following not *possessing,* accompanying not *dismissing,* and meeting the divine in the material instead of *longing for the divine 'out there' in a pre/post-earthly home.*

Section 2 began by noticing that in Jesus's calling of his disciples, following replaced possessing; indeed, as Luke 14:33 makes clear, following is not possible while possessing. Possessing – whether houses, livelihoods, family members, wealth or, in today's neoliberal context, all that we are pressured to consume – holds people back from living the gospel and so has to be let go; but it does not leave a void. It leaves the satisfactions of the life that ensues from following, from being a disciple.

Section 3 gave an account of the difficulties of living out the biblical command to love neighbours, strangers, and enemies and suggested the word 'companionship' as an aid to fulfilling the command. Framed as a verb, 'accompanying' is understood as intrinsically mutual, not unidirectional. To accompany is to refuse to possess another person or people; accompanying demands that differences are honoured, that any conversation is two-way (no one possesses the discourse), and that structures based on possession are resisted and reimagined.

Section 4 rearticulated sacramentality so as to ground the home of humans in the life of God, to overcome once and for all 'the gap of the now' by trusting our bodies to see, hear, smell, taste, touch, and intuit the divine through quotidian, creaturely experiences. To live sacramentally means to discern the sacramental in all of existence. Living in such a way is responsive, reflexive, and fundamentally creative as we meet the divine in materiality; and in its very constructiveness it deconstructs all notions of the earth or anything of it as a possession, as for our 'use'. Sacramentality also affirms our participation in divine intersubjectivity, reminding us that our bodies are part of God's body; and because our bodies are from God, they are not our own (1. Cor 6:19). Living sacramentally reveals that we cannot possess ourselves.

Likewise, the common telos of these disciplines, participation, is also enlivened when expressed as 'participating' – it renders one already active in something bigger than oneself and draws the imagination towards what that might be, shedding the implication of stasis/possession in the noun-form. Conceiving home as 'participating' also brings into yet sharper relief its intersubjective character in the sense of the historic and ongoing interactivity of humans. Home is rendered irreducibly plural and eschatological; it is no longer down to an individual to strive to find, finance, furnish, and fortify their four walls in order to feel a sense of belonging, because they are already participating in home. Participating is impossible to sense 'in the now' without the manifold bodies that have made it possible, the bodies that have shown the Way, broken the bread, named the beauty.

What Then Is Home for a Christian?

Participating by following, accompanying, and living sacramentally orients us in very particular ways towards and within the interrelations that constitute our lives. Recognising such interrelationship is not just a matter of emphasis – noticing the relational aspects of life more and valuing the possession side of things less – rather, living according to the interrelations formed by these three disciplines is in and through itself an eschewal of possession. Home becomes imagined as one part in the network of interrelations that sustains life. Home becomes something which enables one's participation in the specific sorts of relationships that stem from the specific disciplines by which we live – as in Section 2's description of Christian homes as facilitators of the circuitry of discipleship, not assets that benefit individuals.

Throughout history, many Christians have lived in these ways, and the types of housing arrangements that have flowed from their lives are many and varied. 2 Acts tells of local communities in the late first or early second century sharing all they have in common, eating in each other's houses, and loving it. The networks of ascetics formed by the Ammas and Abbas in the Scetes Desert appealed to so many thousands of adherents that Athanasius remarked 'the desert had become a city' (Chryssavgis, 2008: 15). Those desert communities are also thought of as the forerunners of early mediaeval monasticism (Wortley, 2019). Monastic life went on to take many different forms, from small hermitages to large convents; from cloisters to complex community hubs, and a great variety of ways of living in between (Lawrence, 2013). And the past century has seen the birth and growth of – among others – Catholic Worker houses, Indigenous Eco-Villages, Co-Housing collectives, Transition Towns, and multiple idiosyncratic intentional communities – including ones with podcasts (e.g., SACRED, 2024); plus, of course, Emmaus Communities.

But I imagine that for the majority of people reading this argument, as for me nowadays, living 'alternatively' is not currently an option. (For even when it is desired, it might not be possible due to the limits that capitalism imposes on life-forms: for example, some of my friends wanted to form a small intentional community in Ireland but banking rules prohibited it, because while a single person or a couple can get a mortgage, two couples or any other mixture of cohabiters cannot.) The question then becomes what the theology of home proposed here implies for one's housing when it is dependent on a tenancy or a mortgage, or if one is in the fortunate position of owning one's house. How does the premise of 'following replaces possession' work in those circumstances?

Christians can be helped in imagining their housing along the lines of that premise by geographers who have shown, contra the conceptual norms of nationalism and capitalism, that space, because it is known in time, is inexhaustibly mobile and contingent, such that any one place is formed by interrelations – interrelations that stretch from the micro to the global. As Doreen Massey proposes, 'the particularity of any place is, in these terms, constructed not by placing boundaries around it and defining its identity through counter-position to the other which lies beyond, but precisely (in part) through the specificity of the mix of links and interconnections *to* that "beyond"' (1994: 5). What is shed in this view, as in the idea of home as participation in the life of God, is the notion of a home as a fixed, singular, already defined, and barriered to others place. With that loss of stasis also comes the loss of the idea of home as pure origin. Of course, symbiotic human-land relationships where they still exist (or can be reconciled) are deeply nourishing, but that symbiosis is also a massive relational matrix, even as it is felt in specific locales, and so cannot bear the claim that it authenticates 'us' and not 'them'. As Massey says, 'Places viewed this way are open and porous' (1994: 5).

Like many a second-generation migrant, I can attest to the ways that 'home' can both move and not delimit authenticity when it is unbounded in the ways Massey describes. However, such an attestation must be formed in community and in resistance to the dominant culture's perception of one as not belonging (e.g., Irish in England and English in Ireland; each the unwanted party) which is the product of a possessive view of home and a concomitantly racist view of origins. As Ahmed et al. put it, reflecting on the experiences of postcolonial women migrants: 'Being grounded is not necessarily about being fixed; being mobile is not necessarily about being detached' (2003: 1). And yet, as someone who moved twelve times in fifteen years between my late twenties and early forties, nine of them as a result of a landlord evicting me so they could raise the rent, I can also attest to the fact that being at the mercy of rental markets robs one of health, money, time, peace of mind, work not done, vacations not taken, and, of course, a sense of home. So 'mobility' in relation to the question of what a Christian ought to claim as a home must be carefully understood. The nomadism of some indigenous societies is misrepresented when it is thought of as random wandering; nomads were, literally, grounded, there being a deep symbiosis between a set of places and the movement that happened between them. What is helpful when nomadism is accurately imagined is that what is 'mobile' is the interrelations of place, people, land, animals, plants, and all else that is needed for life (Basso, 1996). Mobility is a way of saying that none of these should be thought of as possession.

So for a Christian, even if one 'possesses' the deeds to a house, one's housing is to be held as if in trust, as a locus of politics. It is a kenotic site, formed by the interrelations that arise from the disciplines that constitute participation in the life of God. The key word is perhaps 'open'. Home, when a verb of participating/rejecting possession, has to be held as in an open palm, open to the future, open to the stranger, open to the other, open to the Spirit. However, as bell hooks discerns, such a view of home, while creative and sustaining, comes with a built-in vulnerability: 'For me this space of radical openness is a margin – a profound edge. Locating oneself there is difficult yet necessary. It is not a "safe" place. One is always at risk. One needs a community of resistance' (1989: 19). For Christians, ideally, such a community of resistance comes through church; but as noted in Section 4, many Christians are excluded from or alienated by church. My hope is that the sense of participation that comes through the three disciplines outlined earlier has within itself the imagination of community, whether that is manifested in institutional settings or in alternative communities of faith; how this happens becomes clearer when one imagines participation as a verb: participating. Because 'to home', to reject possession, is to realise the action of God (now) in our lives as a sort of in-built 'homing instinct', perhaps best expressed as: 'abide in me, as I abide in you' (John 15:4).

Participating in the life of God affords such a sense of home in the here-and-now that the appeal of nationalism and capitalism, those ultimately unsatisfactory senses of belonging, can be resisted and, with them, the homelessness they cause. It amounts to a theology of home wherein God is saying to us, and so we have the chance to say to both ourselves and others, 'You are very welcome here.'

References

Bible quotations are from the New Revised Standard Version (1995).

Aalbers, Manuel, ed. (2012). *Subprime Cities: The Political Economy of Mortgage Markets*. London: Wiley.

Adams, Keith. (2022). Tenant State of Mind: How Cost Rental Public Housing Can Reverse the State's Transformation to a Tenant. *Policy Papers*. Dublin: Jesuit Centre for Faith and Justice.

Ahmed, Sara, Castañeda, Claudia, Fortier, Anne-Marie, and Sheller, Mimi, eds. (2003). *Uprootings/Regroundings: Questions of Home and Migration*. London: Routledge.

Anderson, Benedict. (2006). *Imagined Communities*. London: Verso.

Anderson, Gary A. (2023). *That I May Dwell among Them: Incarnation and Atonement in the Tabernacle Narrative*. Grand Rapids, MI: Eerdmans.

Andrews, Emily Snider. (2017). Evangelicals, Modern Worship Music, and the Possibility of Divine-Human Encounter. *Proceedings: North American Academy of Liturgy*, 95–112.

Arnold, Kathleen R. (2004). *Homelessness, Citizenship and Identity*. New York: State University of New York Press.

Backhurst, Stephen. (2011). *Kierkegaard's Critique of Christian Nationalism*. Oxford: Oxford University Press.

Baldovin, John. (2018). The Sacramentality of the Word: An Ecumenical Approach. *Journal of Ecumenical Studies*, 55:2, 224–244.

Basso, Keith H. (1996). *Wisdom Sits in Places: Landscape and Language among the Western Apache*. Albuquerque: University of New Mexico Press.

Bauman, Zygmunt. (2000). *Liquid Modernity*. London: Polity.

Beaton, Rhodora. (2014). *Embodied Words, Spoken Signs: Sacramentality and the Word in Rahner and Chauvet*. Minneapolis, MN: Fortress Press.

Berger, Peter, Berger, Brigitte, and Kellner, Hansfried. (1974). *The Homeless Mind: Modernization and Consciousness*. New York: Random House.

Bernard, Marcel. (2019). Art as Sacrament. *Stellenbosch Theological Journal*, 5:2, 13–28.

Boersma, Hans. (2011). *Heavenly Participation: The Weaving of a Sacramental Tapestry*. Grand Rapid, MI: Eerdmans.

Boeve, Lieven. (2018). Symbols of Who We Are Called to Become: Sacraments in a Secular and Post-Christian Society. *Studia Liturgica*, 48, 147–163.

References

Boff, Leonardo. (1998). *Sacraments of Life, Life of the Sacraments.* Washington, DC: Pastoral Press.

Bouma-Prediger, Steven, and Walsh, Brian. (2008). *Beyond Homelessness: Christian Faith in a Culture of Displacement.* Grand Rapids, MI: Eerdmans.

Brewer, Brian C. (2017). *Martin Luther and the Seven Sacraments: A Contemporary Protestant Reappraisal.* Ada, MI: Baker.

Brown, Raymond E. (1966). *The Gospel according to John I–XII.* Garden City, NY: Doubleday.

Brubaker, Rogers. (2017). *Grounds for Difference.* Cambridge, MA: Harvard University Press.

Buchannan, Deborah. (2011). Vocational Journeys: Moving toward a Vocational and Disruptive Pedagogy. Melanie Harris and Kate Ott, eds., *Faith, Feminism and Scholarship: The Next Generation.* New York: Palgrave Macmillan, pp. 187–196.

Cavanaugh, William T. (2011). *Migrations of the Holy: God, State, and the Political Meaning of the Church.* Cambridge: Eerdmans.

Chauvet, Louis–Marie. (2001). *The Sacraments: The Word of God at the Mercy of the Body.* Collegeville, MN: Liturgical Press. (French original, 1997).

(1995). *Symbol and Sacrament: A Sacramental Reinterpretation of Christian Existence.* Collegeville, MN: Liturgical Press. (French original, 1987).

Chryssavgis, John. (2019). *Creation as Sacrament: Reflections on Ecology and Spirituality* London: T+T Clark.

(2008). *In the Heart of the Desert: The Spirituality of the Desert Fathers and Mothers.* Bloomington, IN: World Wisdom.

Cloke, Paul J. (2010). *Swept-Up Lives? Re-envisioning the Homeless City.* London: Wiley-Blackwell.

(2002). *Rural Homelessness: Issues, Experiences and Policy Responses.* Bristol: Policy Press.

Colonello, Pio. (1999). Homelessness as Heimatlosigkeit? John Abarno, ed., *The Ethics of Homelessness: Philosophical Perspectives.* Amsterdam: Brill, pp. 41–54.

Cooke, Bernard. (1983). *Sacraments & Sacramentality.* Mystic, CT: TwentyThird.

Copeland, M. Shawn. (2018). *Knowing Christ Crucified: The Witness of African American Religious Experience.* New York: Orbis.

Costoya, Manuel Mejido, ed. (2021). *Land of Stark Contrasts: Faith-Based Responses to Homelessness in the United States.* New York: Fordham University Press.

Crisis. (2024). Report. www.crisis.org.uk/about-us/media-centre/rough-sleep ing-rises-by-27-as-the-homelessness-crisis-deepens-across-england/#:~:

text=The%20number%20of%20people%20sleeping,%E2%80%93%20a%20rise%20of%2022%25.

Currie, Thomas Christian. (2016). *The Only Sacrament Left to Us: The Threefold Word of God in the Theology and Ecclesiology of Karl Barth*. Cambridge: James Clarke.

Dominiak, Paul. (2020). 'Participants of the Divine Nature': The Modern Retrieval of Participation. *Reviews in Religion & Theology*, 27, 154–162.

Donahue, John R. (1978). Jesus as the Parable of God in the Gospel of Mark. *Interpretation*, 32:4, 369–386.

Du Mez, Kirstin Kobes. (2021). *Jesus and John Wayne: How White Evangelicals Corrupted a Faith and Fractured a Nation*. New York: Norton.

Duyvendak, Jan Willem. (2011). *The Politics of Home: Belonging and Nostalgia in Western Europe and the United States*. New York: Palgrave Macmillan.

European Commission. (2021). Lisbon Declaration https://ec.europa.eu/social/main.jsp?catId=1061&langId=en#:~:text=Combatting%20homelessness%20%E2%80%93%20a%20priority%20for%20Social%20Europe&text=They%20agreed%20on%20the%20following,to%20a%20permanent%20housing%20solution.

Fiorenza, Elisabeth Schüssler. (1993). *Discipleship of Equals: A Critical Feminist Ekklēsia-ology of Liberation*. London: SCM Press.

Fisher, Lauren B., Overholser, James C., Ridley, Josephine, Braden, Abby, and Rosoff, Cari. (2015). From the Outside Looking In: Sense of Belonging, Depression, and Suicide Risk. *Psychiatry*, 78, 29–41.

Focus Ireland. (2024). Report. www.focusireland.ie/focus-blog/why-are-the-numbers-of-people-homeless-at-record-level-and-what-can-be-done-to-stop-further-increases/#:~:text=Non%20stop%20increase%20in%20adult,did%20just%20a%20decade%20ago.

Francis, Pope. (2015). Laudato Si': On Care for Our Common Home. www.vatican.va/content/francesco/en/encyclicals/documents/papa-francesco_20150524_enciclica-laudato-si.html.

Gafney, Wil. (2011). Parshat Eqev: Neighbors and Strangers, www.wilgafney.com/2011/08/20/parshat-eqev-neighbors-and-strangers/.

Garrigan, Siobhán. (2022). Prayer and Reconciliation. Ashley Cocksworth, ed., *The T+T Clark Handbook of Christian Prayer*. London: Bloomsbury, pp. 601–616.

(2017). The Hermeneutics of Intersubjectivity: A Study of Theologies of Homelessness. Stephan Van Erp, Martin Poulsom, and Lieven Boeve, eds., *Grace, Governance and Globalization*. London: Bloomsbury, pp. 62–76.

(2014). Irish Theology as White Theology: A Case of Mistaken Identity? *Modern Theology*, 30:2, 193–218.

(2010). *The Real Peace Process*. London: Equinox. (Reprint 2014. Abingdon: Routledge).

(2009). Queer Worship. *Theology and Sexuality*, 15:2, 211–230.

(2004). *Beyond Ritual: Sacramental Theology after Habermas*. Abingdon: Ashgate. (Reprint 2017. Abingdon: Routledge).

Gebara, Ivone. (1999). *Longing for Running Water: Ecofeminism and Liberation*. Minneapolis, MN: Fortress Press.

George, Rosemary Marangoly. (1999). *The Politics of Home: Postcolonial Relocations and Twentieth-Century Fiction*. Berkeley: University of California Press.

Goldrick-Kelly, Paul, and Taft, Michael. (2023). Building a Unitary Housing Market: Proposals to End Ireland's Housing Woes. *Policy Papers*. Dublin: Nevin Economic Research Institute. www.nerinstitute.net/sites/default/files/2023-09/NERI%20Long%20Read%20Series%20no%207%20-%20Building%20a%20unitary%20housing%20market%20Sept%202023.pdf.

Gonwa, Janna. (2015). Augustine and Kierkegaard: Eros, Agape, and Neighbour-Love as Ontological Gift. *Toronto Journal of Theology*, 31:1, 84–93.

Gorringe, Timothy. (2002). *A Theology of the Built Environment: Justice, Empowerment, Redemption*. Cambridge: Cambridge University Press.

Hargaden, Kevin. (2023). Where's the Common Good in the Migrant Crisis? *News: 3 March 2023*. Dublin: Jesuit Centre for Faith and Justice. www.jcfj.ie/2023/03/03/wheres-the-common-good-in-the-migrant-crisis/.

(2021). (Irish) Neoliberalism's Ruins: Ghost and Vacant Properties as Signposts of Idolatry. Katie Day and Elise M. Edwards, eds., *The Routledge Handbook of Religion and Cities*. Abingdon: Routledge, pp. 166–181.

Harvey, David. (2005). *A Brief History of Neo-Liberalism*. Oxford: Oxford University Press.

Hastings, Adrian. (1997). *The Construction of Nationhood: Ethnicity, Religion and Nationhood*. Cambridge: Cambridge University Press.

Heidegger, Martin. (1971). *Poetry, Language, Thought*. New York: Harper & Row. (German original, 1951).

hooks, bell. (1989). Choosing the Margin as a Space of Radical Openness. *Framework: The Journal of Cinema and Media*, 36, 15–23.

Hughes, Graham. (2017). *Reformed Sacramentality*. Collegeville, MN: Liturgical Press.

Jennings, Willie James. (2023). *The Bampton Lectures*, Oxford University. Unpublished–personal notes.

(2019). Reframing the World: Toward an Actual Christian Doctrine of Creation. *International Journal of Systematic Theology*, 21:4, 388–407.

(2010). *The Christian Imagination: Theology and the Origins of Race*. New Haven, CT: Yale University Press.

Johnson, Elizabeth A. (2000, June 17). Mary of Nazareth: Friend of God and Prophet. *America: The Jesuit Review*. www.americamagazine.org/faith/2000/06/17/mary-nazareth-friend-god-and-prophet.

Johnson, Sarah and Thiessen, Anneli Loepp. (2023). Contemporary Worship Music as an Ecumenical Liturgical Movement. *Worship: A Journal of Liturgical Studies*, 97, 204–229.

Jong, Jae-Woong. (2020). The Sacramentality of Preaching: A Sacramental Theological Approach to Preaching as the Word of God. *Theology and Praxis*, 70, 61–92.

Kavanagh, Patrick. (2003). *A Poet's Country: Selected Prose*, edited by Antoinette Quinn. Dublin: Lilliput. (Original 1967).

Keenan, James F. and McGreevy, Mark. (2019). *Street Homelessness and Catholic Theological Ethics*. New York: Orbis Books.

Koenig, Sarah. (2008). This Is My Daily Bread: Toward a Sacramental Theology of Evangelical Worship. *Worship: A Journal of Liturgical Studies*, 82, 141–161.

Lane, David. (2023). *Global Neoliberal Capitalism and the Alternatives: From Social Democracy to State Capitalisms*. Bristol: Bristol University Press.

Lawrence, C. H. (2013). *Medieval Monasticism: Forms of Religious Life in Europe in the Middle Ages*. New York: Routledge.

Lee, Barrett, Shinn, Marybeth, and Culhane, Dennis. (2021). Homelessness as a Moving Target. *The Annals of the American Academy of Political and Social Science*, 693:1, 8–26.

Longenecker, Richard, ed. (1996). *Patterns of Discipleship in the New Testament*. Grand Rapids, MI: Eerdmans.

Ludden, Jennifer. (2023, December 15). Homelessness in the U.S. Hit a Record High Last Year as Pandemic Aid Ran Out. *NPR*. www.npr.org/homelessness-affordable-housing-crisis-rent-assistance.

Marrocco, Mary R. N. (2000). Participation in the Divine Life in St. Augustine's *De Trinitate* and Selected Contemporary Homiletic Discourses. *Toronto School of Theology Dissertations*. Toronto: University of St. Michael's College.

Massey, Doreen. (1994). *Space, Place, and Gender*. Minneapolis: University of Minnesota Press.

Mbembe, Achille. (2019). *Necropolitics*. Chapel Hill, NC: Duke University Press.

McCarraher, Eugene. (2019). *The Enchantment of Mammon: How Capitalism Became the Religion of Modernity*. Cambridge, MA: Harvard University Press.

McConnell, Gail. (2021). Interview. https://static1.squarespace.com/static/5daeee9a317b5e0d4e2c35c3/t/6036ba87da3d910b74dab4fc/1614199432386/Corrymeela+Podcast+interview+with+Gail+McConnell+Reflection+Questions+and+Transcript.pdf.

McFadyen, Alistair. (2013). On Having Enemies: Terror, Torture, Theology ... Policing. www.academia.edu/1819337/On_having_enemies_Terror_Torture_Theology_Policing.

McFague, Sallie. (2021). *A New Climate for Christology: Kenosis, Climate Change, and Befriending Nature*. Minneapolis, MN: Fortress Press.

(1993). *The Body of God: An Ecological Theology*. Minneapolis, MN: Fortress Press.

McGahern, John. (2005). *Memoir*. London: Faber and Faber.

McGinnis, Kelsey Kramer. (2023). Corporate Worship: We Could Sing of His Love Forever: Investors Are Counting on It. *Christianity Today*, 67:4, 26–27.

McLoughlin, Thomas. (2022). *In Christ Now Meet Both East and West*. Collegeville, MN: Liturgical Press.

Meecham, H. G. (1935). *The Epistle of Diognetus*. Manchester: Manchester University Press.

Mercedes, Anna. (2022). Kenosis in Catastrophe. *The Kenarchy Journal*, 4, 1–11.

Mulligan, Suzanne. (2023). Homelessness: Some Theological Reflections. *Studies: An Irish Theological Quarterly*, 112, 439–451.

Mylonas, Harris and Tudor, Maya. (2023). *Varieties of Nationalism: Communities, Narratives, Identities*. Cambridge: Cambridge University Press.

Nixon, David. (2013). *Stories from the Street: A Theology of Homelessness*. London: Routledge.

O'Sullivan, Eoin. (2022). *Key Elements in Homelessness Strategies to End Homelessness by 2030: A Discussion Paper*. Luxembourg: European Union Publications Office.

(2020). *Reimagining Homelessness for Policy and Practice*. Chicago, IL: University of Chicago Press.

Ortner, Sherry B. (2011). On Neoliberalism, *Anthropology of This Century*. http://aotcpress.com/articles/neoliberalism/.

Parekh, Serena. (2016). *Refugees and the Ethics of Forced Displacement*. London: Routledge.

Pauw, Amy Plantinga. (2017). *Church in Ordinary Time: A Wisdom Ecclesiology*. Grand Rapids, MI: Eerdmans.

Perry, Samuel and Whitehead, Andrew. (2020). *Taking America Back for God: Christian Nationalism in the United States*. New York: Oxford University Press.

Peukert, Helmut. (1986). *Science, Action, and Fundamental Theology: Toward a Theology of Communicative Action*. Boston, MA: MIT Press.

Portugal, Elsen. (2020). Musical Worship: The New Sacrament? The Contemporary Meaning of the Musical Worship Moment among Brazilian Baptist Churches. *Great Commission Research Journal*, 11:2, 52–87.

Power, David N. (1998). *Sacraments: The Language of God's Giving*. New York: Crossroad

Rahner, Karl. (1963). *The Church and the Sacraments*. New York: Herder and Herder.

Rahner, Karl. (1978). *Foundations of Christian Faith*. New York: Seabury Press.

Ramirez Kidd, José E. (1999). *Alterity and Identity in Israel: The 'Ger' in the Old Testament*. Berlin: Walter de Gruyter.

Rieger, Jeorg. (2018). *Jesus vs. Caesar: For People Tired of Serving the Wrong God*. Nashville, TN: Abingdon.

Rosen, Matt. (2019). On Neighborly and Preferential Love in Kierkegaard's *Works of Love*. *Journal of Philosophy and Scripture*, 8, 1–20.

Ross, Susan. (1998). *Extravagant Affections: A Feminist Sacramental Theology*. London: Bloomsbury.

Ruether, Rosemary Radford. (1993). *Sexism and God-Talk: Toward a Feminist Theology*. Boston, MA: Beacon Press.

SACRED, a podcast. (2024). www.youtube.com/watch?v=yJHAzfKL3RQ.

Sacrosanctum concilium. (1962). The Holy See's Documents from Vatican II. www.vatican.va/archive/hist_councils/ii_vatican_council/documents/vat-ii_const_19631204_sacrosanctum-concilium_en.html.

Schillebeeckx, Edward. (1963). *Christ the Sacrament of Encounter with God*. London: Sheed and Ward.

Sennett, Richard. (1990). *The Conscience of the Eye: The Design and Social Life of Cities*. New York: Norton.

Simon Community Ireland. (2022). *Report: Hidden Homelessness*. www.simon.ie/wp-content/uploads/2022/09/Simon-Communities-of-Ireland_Hidden-Homeless-Poll.pdf.

Smith, Anthony D. (1998). *Nationalism and Modernism*. London: Routledge.
Spivak, Gayatri Chakravorty. (2009). Nationalism and the Imagination. *Lectora*, 15, 75–98.
Stivers, Laura. (2011). *Disrupting Homelessness: Alternative Christian Approaches*. Minneapolis, MN: Fortress Press.
Streeck, Wolfgang. (2016). *How Will Capitalism End?* London: Verso.
Theissen, Gerd. (1978). *Sociology of Early Palestinian Christianity*. Minneapolis, MN: Fortress.
UNHCR. (2024). *Annual Report*. www.unrefugees.org/refugee-facts/statistics/#:~:text=Global%20Trends%20At%2Da%2DGlance,43.4%20million%20refugees.
 (2000). *The State of the World's Refugees 2000: Fifty Years of Humanitarian Action*. Oxford: Oxford University Press.
Van der Tol, Marietta. (2024). *Constitutional Intolerance: The Fashioning of the 'Other' in Europe's Constitutional Repertoires*. Cambridge: Cambridge University Press.
Van der Tol, Marietta and Gorski, Philip. (2022). Secularisation as the Fragmentation of the Sacred and of Sacred Space. *Religion, State and Society*, 50:5, 495–512.
Veeneman, Mary. (2017). Feminism and Womanism. Justin Holcomb and David Johnson, eds., *Christian Theologies of the Sacraments: A Comparative Introduction*. New York: New York University Press, pp. 352–365.
Viefhues-Bailey, Ludger. (2023). *No Separation: Christians, Secular Democracy, and Sex*. New York: Columbia University Press.
Ward, Graham. (2009). *The Politics of Discipleship*. Grand Rapids, MI: Baker.
Westfield, N. Lynne. (2001). *Dear Sisters: A Womanist Practice of Hospitality*. Michigan: Pilgrim Press.
Williams, Rowan. (2016). *Being Disciples: Essentials of the Christian Life*. London: SPCK.
Wortley, John. (2019). *An Introduction to the Desert Fathers*. Cambridge: Cambridge University Press.
Zizioulas, John. (1985). *Being as Communion: Studies in Personhood and the Church*. Crestwood, NY: St Vladimir's Seminary Press.

Acknowledgements

For their support of this project during its long gestation, I thank Marwa Al-Sabouni, Phil Garrigan, Colin Graham, Ron Grimes, Selina Guinness, Joel Hanisek, Melanie Ross, David Shepherd, emilie townes, Ludger Viefhues-Bailey, and Christiana Zenner.

I would also like to thank my former companions at Emmaus, my students past and present, and all my colleagues at Exeter, where the project was first imagined – especially Tim Gorringe, David Horrell, and Mark Wynn.

Aspects of the project benefitted from feedback at presentations, and I thank those who invited me – Karen Kilby (The Society for the Study of Theology), Ulrich Schmiedel (Edinburgh and Oxford), Stephan Van Erp (Njimegen), and Graham Ward (Oxford).

And most of all, for their great help in bringing this project onto the page, I thank: Jacob Erickson, Sinéad Garrigan, Kevin Hargaden, Rachel Muers, Sam Stoney, Danielle Tumminio Hansen, and the whole team at Cambridge University Press.

Cambridge Elements =

Christian Doctrine

Rachel Muers
University of Edinburgh

Rachel Muers is Professor of Divinity at the University of Edinburgh. Her publications include *Keeping God's Silence* (2004), *Living for the Future* (2008), and *Testimony: Quakerism and Theological Ethics* (2015). She is co-editor of *Ford's The Modern Theologians: An Introduction to Christian Theology Since 1918*, 4th edition (2024). She is a former president of the Society for the Study of Theology.

Ashley Cocksworth
University of Roehampton

Ashley Cocksworth is Reader in Theology and Practice at the University of Roehampton, UK. He is the author of *Karl Barth on Prayer*; *Prayer: A Guide for the Perplexed*; and (with David F. Ford) *Glorification and the Life of Faith*. His edited volumes include *T&T Clark Handbook of Christian Prayer*; *Karl Barth: Spiritual Writings*; and (with Rachel Muers), *Ford's The Modern Theologians: An Introduction to Christian Theology since 1918*.

Simeon Zahl
University of Cambridge

Simeon Zahl is Professor of Christian Theology at the University of Cambridge and a Fellow of Jesus College.

About the Series

Elements in Christian Doctrine brings creative and constructive thinking in the field of Christian doctrine to a global audience within and beyond the academy. The series demonstrates the vitality of Christian doctrine and its capacity to engage with contemporary questions.

Cambridge Elements≡

Christian Doctrine

Elements in the Series

Life after Death after Marx
Simon Hewitt

A Theology of Home in a Time of Homelessness
Siobhán Garrigan

A full series listing is available at: www.cambridge.org/ECDR

For EU product safety concerns, contact us at Calle de José Abascal, 56–1°,
28003 Madrid, Spain or eugpsr@cambridge.org.

www.ingramcontent.com/pod-product-compliance
Lightning Source LLC
LaVergne TN
LVHW020351260326
834688LV00045B/1671